FOUR YEARS IN TIBET

FOUR YEARS IN TIBET

Ahmad Shah

GIAN PUBLISHING HOUSE
New Delhi-110002

GIAN PUBLISHING HOUSE
4C Ansari Road
New Delhi 110002

First published 1906
Reprinted 1991

ISBN 81-212-0392-9

PRINTED IN INDIA

Published by Mrs Gayatri Garg for Gian Publishing House, New Delhi, and printed at Goyal Offset Printers, Delhi.

CONTENTS.

PAGE.

Preface

CHAPTER I.

My journey to Cashmere and thence to Lower Tibet 1

CHAPTER II.

Mr. Notovitch and his find ... 28

Eastern diplomacy ... 30

The great master Renan ... 32

CHAPTER III.

History 34

CHAPTER IV.

Government 37

CHAPTER V.

The country 41

CHAPTER VI.

The people 44

CHAPTER VII.

Occupation 47

PAGE.

CHAPTER VIII.

Birth 51

CHAPTER IX

Marriage 55

CHAPTER X.

Physic 59

CHAPTER XI.

Burial 62

CHAPTER XII.

Sports, amusements and festivals 65

CHAPTER XIII.

Curious customs 70

CHAPTER XIV.

Why are foreigners forbidden to enter Tibet? 73

CHAPTER XV.

History of the Buddhist religion in Tibet 76

PREFACE.

Although the first part of my book "My journey to Kashmere and thence to Lower Tibet" is a sufficient introduction to the complete volume, I should not depart from the orthodox custom of writing a preface.

In October, 1897, when I stepped upon English soil coming fresh from Lower Tibet I was at once interviewed by a representative of the "Daily Chronicle" regarding the then burning subject of the day, the "Landour outrage". I communicated to him my opinion of the matter which was widely reported by English and some of the Indian papers. This was my first introduction to the English public and I continued to receive letters and invitations from many persons who were interested in the subject, to give them more information about Tibet and the people who live in it.

I could not avail myself of these opportunities until November 26th when at the special request of the Secretary of the Martinue Club, in connection with the Manchester College Oxford, I read a paper before the Club, on the social and religious customs of the Tibetans. I illustrated my subject with a number of lantern slides which I had made for the purpose, and was pleasantly surprised to notice that my English audience evinced a very marked interest in the address, and warmly appreciated the illusrations.

On January 20th, 1898, I delivered an address at Wandsworth, London, on the same subject illustrated by means of 75 slides which were prepared from the water-colour drawings I made and photographs I took in Tibet, and again on March 16th before the "Oxford Natural History Society" at the request of the president, A. M. Bell, Esqr., M. A. Then I was requested by the Secretary of the Y. M. C. A. at Oxford to deliver a like lecture which I did on March 25th.

The amount of encouragement I received during that sojourn, backed up by kindly suggestions from people of note, made me bold enough to conceive the idea of bringing out a book for the English reading public. Later I disclosed my plan to Dr. Leider, Librarian of the Indian Institute at Oxford, and he said it was a pity that while chance travellers spending a few weeks in Tibet on business, or in pursuit of pleasure professed to know so much of a foreign and inaccessible country, I who spent four long years in the midst of the people, living like any other native among them should hesitate to give an account of that interesting country, and people. He would prefer me to any such authors. I need hardly say how encouraged I felt at the learned doctor's words. He also suggested to me that I should first go through the existing works upon Tibet in order to ascertain what additional original information I could give.

Accordingly I read Cunningham, Captain Taylor, Huc, Drew, Ramsay, Knight, Bower, Waddell and a few others. Waddell's is an exceedingly able work, but is interesting only to one who seeks information upon religion. Cunningham's is the most important work for general readers. It gives general information and is written by one who was well versed with the subject, but it is out of print and out of date. Drew and Ramsay supply better information than others but it is mostly about Ladakh. These four works have however proved very useful to me in compiling my book. In fact they have much shortened my labour. My diary was compiled when I had no idea of any possibility of my writing about the country and the people who live in it. But in England I was advised to record my evidence in order to refute the assertions of Notovich, and I have used my diary which is very copious and extensive in writing what was to satisfy my friends and myself.

Thus the material in hand was arranged under separate headings subject to further re-arrangement, classification, improvements and necessary corrections. But unexpected circumstances compelled my immediate return to India and I had to give up all possible hope of publication of the book in England. Here in India I asked several friends to go through the manuscript and make necessary corrections which to a certain extent they kindly did but the opinion as to its publication was not so encouraging as in England. I, therefore, placed the manuscript amongst my other curious things of Tibet.

After seven long years in 1904, I happened to visit a well-known publishing firm of Benares, and in the course of my conversation with the proprietor I mentioned my manuscript to him. He was much interested and on his request I submitted it to him with the water-color sketches. After perusal he informed me that his firm was quite willing to bring out the book.

I agreed to the proposal on the clear understanding that I had no time at my disposal to apply myself for further revision of the manuscript and I handed over my manuscript to him as it was. This is the history of the following pages which are now given to the public.

In conclusion I may add that this is only a venture, but I hope it will be received with some sympathy by people of superior talent.

Hamirpore, U. P.
1906.

AHMAD SHAH.

ERRATA.

Page	*line*	*for*	*read.*
1	2	Mr.	Mrs.
,,	4	strat	start
2	25	on	an
4	40	or	for
6	19	though	through
10	25	persen	person
11	38	1,300	11,300
12	2	exceeding	exceedingly
13	32	orefathers	forefathers
15	30	the Kharboo	Kharboo
19	6	H	He
20	13	enial	denial
18	6	convents	convent
11	7	strangers	stranger
21	Lines 1, 2 and 3 are to be ommitted.		
22	5	napkinsr	napkins
24	1	some	some portions
28	8	critica	critical
39	1	crimiana	criminal
51	18	deas	ideas
57	31	ideas to	ideas.
60	28	vinerial	venerial
63	40	was a	was
66	29	real	rea-
,,	39	too	toe
68	14	is	is lion

CHAPTER I-

MY JOURNEY TO CASHMERE

AND

THENCE TO LOWER TIBET.

It was on the 20th of March 1894, a friend with whom I was staying at Banda, received a telegram from Ajmere to say that Mr. Andrews of America and Pandita Rama Bai wanted to see him at Agra the next day. It was already nine o'clock at night and there were only two hours before the train was to strat. I determined to accompany my friend. We hastily packed for the journey, started at once, and reached Jhansi the next morning where we changed for Agra. Unfortunately it was the season for some great Hindu pilgrimage and the trains were crammed from roof to floor with passengers who were hastening on. We were to travel second class, but on that day there were no second class carriages provided, so we entered a first which was almost empty—there being in it only one Parsee gentleman who was engaged in perusing the columns of the great Anglo-Indian daily, the "Pioneer."

An interesting story of a European cremation was going the round of the papers at that time. A civilian of note in Meerut had willed to be cremated instead of being buried, and the ceremony which had been performed created a great sensation.

A cremation is a very common thing in India. Every Hindu is cremated. But for a European to be cremated on Indian soil is a rare event. Of course in France or in England no one would be startled by such a method of disposing of the dead; in those countries in fact we read of Christian cremation as a Christian rite.

Both of us were interested in the story and the Parsee gentleman having offered the paper to us, I read it through and then cast a glance over the advertisement column. My eye was attracted by the words: "WANTED, a medical man of experience for Leh in Ladakh."

I was out of employment; but as my wife had just recovered from a long illness and was still at Banda for a change, I was not just then prepared to accept a post. But some how or other I thought it worth while just to try for it. I, therefore, drafted an application while the train was in motion posted it at once, to see what would come of it. I thought there would be sufficient time to consider the matter before I received the reply.

In due time we reached Agra. When we arrived we found, to our great vexation that it was raining heavily. It was night time, and we drove to the Northbrook Hotel to find out if the ladies above mentioned were there. They had come, and we were to see them on the morrow. That day and a few others we spent in their company visiting all the notable sights of the city, the Taj, Fort, Sikandra and Aitmad-ud-daulah. The dark labyrinth in the fort, a sort of catacomb miniature, interested the Pandita most, as it is associated by tradition with some of the most ghastly stories of the varied cruelties inflicted upon those members of the female sex, who enjoyed the ignominious luxury of being the inmates of the Harem. Perhaps it displayed "the woes of the Harem" and we returned to Banda with much food for thought.

I little thought so soon to receive a reply to my half-serious application; nor indeed did I except it to be favourably considered; but on the 8th of April, a letter reached me from Dr. Deane, the Residency Surgeon, Cashmere, which informed me that I had been selected out of the candidates for the post and that I was to report myself with all speed at Srinagar. I was not prepared for this haste, my wife was still an invalid and almost all my friends being against the plan, I was about to decline the offer, unless an extension of time was allowed.

At this juncture, a sensation was created in English and Indian papers by the news of the notable "find" by Notovitch the Russian traveller, at the convent of Hemis, of a hitherto unknown manuscript of a Tibetan version of the Life of Christ. The interest of this MS. was that it dealt with the period between the twelfth and the thirtieth years of our Lord's life. Some doubted, some affirmed the *bonafides* of the discovery.

An assertion that our Master disappeared at so early on age from the land of Judæa and came to the East, to India, in quest of knowledge, and spent over fifteen years there with the Brahmans, sounded strange to ears that were accustomed to hear of the coming to Judæa of the "wise men of the East" to pay tribute to the rising Sun of Righteousness. I was filled with a desire to ascertain the truth or falsehood of the assertion. When I came to know that Hemis is a place only twenty miles from Leh, I made up my mind to go there, despite all the objections my friends could make, whatever the inconveniences I might have to put up with. There was, in regard to my wife, one solace and that a very substantial one; she was in the house of my friend, whose mother and wife were also there. In leaving her with them I was sure that I was leaving her in very good hands, and my mind was released from a great deal of anxiety, and separation from her, cost me less than it would otherwise have done.

I started from Banda on the 16th of April and went direct to Rawalpindi through Cawnpore, Lucknow, Saharanpore and Lahore. In Lahore, there lived close to the railway station some relatives of mine. I was obliged to wait here about two hours; but as I expected opposition from these relatives, and feared lest they should overcome my inclination, and bring forward reasons against the expediency of my move I thought it safer not to see them at all and proceeded till I reached Rawalpindi on the 19th.

The Indian is a home-loving man and is naturally averse to emigration. The joint family system is of Indian origin; people huddle together in one house, live together, cook together and eat together. No one should leave the home and hearth in quest of health, wealth or any other blessing. The spirit of enterprise is not natural to the people of the country. "Half a loaf at home is better than a whole one abroad" is a well-known Hindi proverb illustrating the domestic bent of the Indian mind. A family feels it the greatest calamity when one of its members goes far away from the home circle. Under the powerful influence of education and Western ideas, Indians force their way into other countries—as a way to glory—leaving behind a cloud of gloom to settle over the group at home. It is not possible for a western mind to realise the unspeakable misery and agony that is suffered by the female relations of young Indian students going to England. It is something like the feelings of parents who see their dear son going into battle.

Having reached Rawalpindi, I had there to bid farewell to the railway. The Tonga and the Ekka were the only conveyances in use for travelling to Cashmere. But as the road at this time was unusually bad and one had to get down at intervals to walk in the more difficult places, I was advised to take the Ekka, though less convenient and more jolty, for I could then take all my luggage with me and not leave it behind as I should have to do had I travelled by Tonga. I accordingly hired two ekkas one for myself and the other for my luggage, and at once started for Murree, where I arrived early next morning.

After taking a little rest, I was able to induce my companions to proceed, till at 11 we reached the next station, Phugwari, and the descent having commenced here the journey was comparatively easy. We had by this time travelled over 50 miles from Rawalpindi without any considerable break and without needing a change of horses to replace those that had to ascend a height of 5000 ft. dragging much luggage. The horses thongh lean and ill-fed are used to this labour and are not easily wearied by distance or load; habit has developed in them strength and patience to an unusual degree.

On the 21st we travelled from Phugwari to Kohala. Here is one of the most picturesque birdges over the Jhelum river which is the boundary line between the British territory and the Cashmere state. On this side of the bridge the British and on the other side the Cashmere tax Collecter is stationed.

After breakfasting we left Kohala and had only travelled two miles via Dolai when we found our path so very bad on account of recent rains, that we had to break up our Ekka into its component parts to be carried by men over some hilly height in order to reach the main road. This unusual feat had to be performed some four times and reminded us of a Hindi proverb "Some times the cart upon the boat and sometimes the boat upon the cart." At four o'clock we reached the end of our two miles journey. At the place we now reached, called Domel, I was employed as Surgeon in 1887. The road was being made at this time under the charge of Mr. Alex. Atkinson, the Engineer; there was a very big workshop here, which has now given place to a very comfortable and necessary "Dak bangla"—resting place—by the road side. I pressed on without halting here, till we reached the other station, Garhi, in the dusk of the evening. Here I spent the night in the "Dak bangla" and the horses and men had sufficient time for rest and refreshment. The next morning we again started. The journey was very difficult that day, more so than that of the previous day, forty-eight miles of mountainous road on an Ekka with a single horse. We thus passed three stations. Every third or fourth mile we had to break up our Ekkas to be carried some distance over impassable land, and then to adjust them again. While journeying we were much alarmed to hear of a fatal accident which had happened that very day. An English traveller's Ekka had slipped down a precipice, the khansama was drowned and the Ekka with the horse carried away by the torrent beneath.

The next day no more rain fell and the road became less dangerous. It was being repaired, but Nature was at war with the poor labourers. Before they had been able to clear a furlong of the road, huge blocks of stone, yielding to the ice water and rain torrents falling over the road, blocked the way for a mile. There was continual disappointment and loss of labour. And despite all efforts to the contrary even the post was delayed.

We reached Ori and started again during rain. Our Ekka wala, who was accustomed to all sorts of accidents and dangers, was full of stories about such things. All along he kept pointing out to me the place where an ekka fell or a Tonga was upset, or a horse slipped, or a man was drowned. The road was associated with ghastly accidents. It is a dangerous road and very narrow. On one side rises the inhospitable mountain, on the other yawns a river's deep abyss of death. If two ekkas or tongas approach from oppsite directions, the one nearest the river is in danger. If the horse shies or any accident happens to the wheel, the conveyance and everything in it is hurled below. On the river side stones have been placed to make the road safer, but this has not been done all along.

On the 23rd of April, 1894, we reached Rampur, and from this place onward like difficulties continually beset us. We left Rampur on the 24th and reached Bara Mula at noon. We had not to break up our Ekkas that day, but the road all along had become, on account of rain, a muddy river; the Ekkas, the horses and ourselves were smeared with dirt, and everything about us wore a muddy aspect. This was the end of our Ekka journey and we parted with the Ekka wallas, having paid them handsomely for their services and company. From thence onwards we swore fealty to the boatmen and put ourselves at their disposal. At Bara Mula we hired a boat, and I tried hard to persuade the boatmen to start on their way to Srinagar at once, but they were hesitating. The reason for this was that only two days previously an Englishman who was in a hurry to start in spite of bad weather was drowned. The wind on the lake was strong and the boat had upset. After much ado, I succeeded in coaxing them to start, giving them an hour to get ready.

It was on the 24th of April and at 5 o'clock in the evening that our boat set out or Srinagar, but we had hardly gone a mile when the wind set in and the boat was in danger. We put back to shore with some difficulty and there the boatmen tied the boat to a tree and I was left to reflect on my haste, which had been so unwelcome to the boatmen.

An elderly looking boatman told me, with a significant look, that he was in the right in resisting my wishes, for it was not a suitable time to start and that we would have to remain there for the whole night. I knew "there was a time for silence." At midnight the sky was again clear and I again tried to take advantage of the good nature of these boatmen to induce them to start. They seemed inclined to resist, but my knowledge of the cowardliness of these boatmen gave me the courage to threaten them into compliance. We started and reached *Sopur* early in the morning, Here I hired eight more boatmen, for the weather was precarious. I had now fourteen men upon my boat. With fourteen oarsmen, the boat flew rapidly over the surface of the lake and we found ourselves in Srinagar at 5 in the evening of the 25th. Soon after I found myself with an old friend and school-mate, Gideon, in the Mission Hospital. On the 26th, I reported my arrival to the Residency Surgeon. He gave me a letter of introduction to Captain Godfrey who was at Chashma Shahi. He told me that I was to wait in Srinagar for two months as the road to Ladakh was quite blocked, and that I would have to get warmer clothing which the Ladakh weather required.

I felt sorry, at first, for the haste with which I had left India, for I was not to reach my place of destination for two months. But then these thoughts disappeared when I sat down to read the newspapers, and found that the supposed find of Notovitch had made a deep impression upon the religious press. The Hindus, the Arayas, the Theosophists and the anti-Christian writers dwelt on the subject with exultation, asserting that even the founder of Christianity had to sit at the feet of Indian sages, and all that he had taught was only a reflection of the wisdom of the Orient. My enthusiasm was once more fired and I was filled with a desire to come to the right conclusion, and to make a personal and independent inquiry. I was open to conviction and was rather predisposed in favour of Notovitch, and attached very little importance to the utterances of his detractors. In Cashmere, I saw two Christian missionary brothers—well-known medical men of the Church of England—Drs. Arthur and Earnest Neve, who practise their healing art with such tact and skill in Cashmere that, from the Maharaja to the poorest peasant, all acknowledge it with gratitude. They work in the spirit of their Master and prepare a way for Him in the hearts of their patients. I am glad to own that once I too had the privilege of working under Dr. Arthur Neve in that very hospital in Cashmere.

Here I also met Mr. Knowles of the Church Missionary Society and asked his opinion about Notovitch's discovery. He told me that he had already ascertained from the Leh Missionaries that the whole affair was a veritable hoax, and that Notovitch had never been even in the vicinity of Leh. I could not credit it. I thought that it was simply impossible that in this enlightened age a gentleman could ever be capable of such a lie. As it was more probable that missionaries being predisposed against the find should be prejudiced against Notovitch.

I, however, continued to spend my time in Srinagar and live in my watery dwelling, the boat. One day as I was walking along the Munshi Bag, I met a few persons wearing long pigtails down their backs. I took them for Chinese. I drew near them and was surprised to discover that one of them could speak Punjabi. I took advantage of this to enter into conversation with them. I asked them whence they came and what had brought them there, and was exceedingly glad to learn that they came from Leh and were at this time with a Kushuk. I learnt later what a kushuk was in reality, but at this moment was content to think that he was some great religious personage in Buddhism. I took my new acquaintance to my boat and there treated him to tea and other refreshment and then, as if in recompense for my hospitality, I asked to be introduced to his Kushuk.

He consented to the proposal and assured me that if I called on him the next day, I would see the Kushuk in Basant-Bag. I thanked him and the next day I was in the presence of his grace, reverance, or holiness or all together. The Kushuk I found seated upon a chair placed upon a pretty and costly *qalin* (carpet) on which a Tibetan dog kept guard, who seeing a stranger like me of questionable sanctity began to make a fuss. The Kushuk quieted him, shook hands with me and made me sit upon another chair close to his. While these preliminaries were being gone though I found out that the Kushuk could also speak a little Urdu intermingled with Punjabi.*

Here was my opportunity. He was very communicative and I, very inquisitive. I moderately fathomed him and extorted from him as much as was advisable at our first

---

* This Kushuk is a man of great importance. He is known by the name of Bakula and is the head of the monastery of Ispatak where our friend Notovitch so unwisely broke one of his legs. Kushuk Bakula, the son of the Raja of Zaniskar, is the very man who helped Captain Ramsay in preparing the dictionary of the Westren Tibetan dialect. He is a man of established fame as an acute scholar of his religion, was educated in Lassa and can rise in his line to anything except the position of Great Lama, the infallible pope of the Buddhist world. Throughout Lower Tibet he has the reputation of being the soundest of scholars. He owns landed property in Cashmere and had come to Cashmere on business. Ha was ill-treated by a certain police officer of the State, and Bakula had, therefore, to lodge a complaint against him before the Maharaja. Once before he had come to Cashmere to pay his respects to Lord Roberts, the then Commander-in-Chief, who had come on a pleasure trip to Cashmere. I have seen a photo of Bakula in Lama costume in a group in the University museum at Oxford.

This Kushuk is unfortunately looked upon now a days with disfavour in Lower Tibet. People have lost somewhat of their confidence in him. For, according to their strict views of monastic life, a Kushuk, who is an incarnation, should not take any very active part in worldly affairs as this Kushuk does. And, perhaps, for this reason he has lost his chances in Lassa. He is afraid to go there lest the Grand Lama shauld have him murdered or otherwise severely dealt with. He was a young man of about 25, very handsome, with a prominent and broad forehead, the index of intelligence and wisdom. His winters he spends in Zaniskar and his summers in Ispituk Monastery.

acquaintance. To my questions, whether and how much he knew of Isa, whether there was among them any independent knowledge of him, whether he knew of any Tibetan or Pali book upon his Life, work or teaching, he answered in a very frank and honest way that all they knew of Isa was through the missionaries of Leh, who often visited the fairs round about the monasteries in their preaching tours, and, so far as his knowledge extended, he was not aware of any work of this nature in their language in all the sacred literature of their country. I asked him about the libraries in their convents, and the nature of the books therein. He said that there were certain books that are common to almost all convents as for instance the books on the life of Buddha and other religious books, transcripts from Lassa originals. But that there was a set of books quite peculiar to every convent. These were the lives of the local monks, their sermons and commentaries which each one, as he completes his course, writes and makes over to his successor to be the private property of the monastery where he lived, moved and had his being.

Now arrived the time for my interlocutor's devotions and it was but just that he should enjoy it to his heart's content. It was my first acquaintance and I did not like to worry him lest I should prejudice him against me. We parted. He noted down my name in his pocket-book and assured me of a second and extended interview with him in Leh. *

After my interview with the Kushuk, I felt a little disappointed and began to doubt the good faith of the statement of Notovitch in regard to his discovery. But then I could not at once accuse the Biographer of the Great Tsar of lie ; he was no ordinary man, he was the author of several works and, *prima facie*, I thought him morally incapable of a flat lie in the daylight of history and civilization. Again, I said to myself that, after all, it might be a living illustration of what Sadi of Shiraz, himself a traveller round the world, declared,

جهاندیده بسیار گوید دروغ

"One who has seen the world utters much falsehood ;"

and again, چه دلاورست دزدے که بکف چراغ دارد

"Daring is the thief who goes about with a light upon his palm."

I did not mind either Sadi or Bakula or Notovitch. I was near Leh and was to ascertain for myself what was the actual truth. First of all I devoted my time to reading modern books upon the religion, people and land of Tibet as an introduction to my inquiry. If I came to

* By the way, I have mentioned a chair and a pocket-book in connection with his holiness, the Kushuk. Lest any one should think it strange, for a Tibetan monk to indulge in this sort of luxury, let it be known to my readers that Kushuk Bakula has several times come to Cashmere, lived for months in Jummu, travelled through the principal towns of the Punjab, has seen much of the modern ways of intercourse and, therefore, whenever he has to see any one who is not unused to European luxuries, he always offers him a chair, and I was but little surprised in my last interview with him that he had also adopted visiting cards, written by hand. The system of visiting cards is in vogue with the Chinese as well, but Bakula has learned many modern ways either from the English or the educated natives of India. This explains the use of the pocket book and discloses the intelligence of the Kushuk, in imitating the useful manners of the foreigners against which his less liberal-minded countrymen are unwisely prejudiced.

hear of any men coming from Leh, I saw them to get as much information as I could regarding the people, their manners, their religion, their ceremonies and their language, and found them very interesting. I began to pick up such of their common expressions as were serviceable to me, as for instance, *Ir yon* (come thither). *Soun* (be gone) *Galayuth* (are you well) and so on. My diary began to swell with these additions.

April had passed and May too. Cashmere had "renewed her youth like an eagle." The season was lustily pleasant. The trees, the offspring of Nature, were beginning to put on their eye-pleasing green apparel. Apple, pear, nut, pomegranate and *Bihi* (quince) had just dropped their blossoms to let the new embryo fruit peep out of its luxurious surrounding to develop into something "good for food and a delight to the eyes." *Khubánis* (appricots) were half raw, *Shahtoot* (mulberry) almost ripe, grapes were yet sour to make fit only into delicious sauce, *Badam* (almonds) were raw but were cooked with meat. *Aluchas* (plums) had acquired the golden yellow tinge. The scene around was as of fairy land.

" This day dame Nature seemed in love,
The lusty sap began to move,
Fresh juice did stirth' embracing vines
And birds had drawn their valentines."

The immortal *Urfi* the most profound, deep and imaginative among the Persian poets has expressed himself about the scenes of Cashmere.

هر سوخته جانے که به کشمیر در آید
گر مرغ کباب است که به بال و پر آید

" Every burnt soul that has come to Cashmere even if it be a roasted fowl, regains its feather and down."

There were daily arriving three or four new European travellers in Cashmere.

The Residency office, when the heat of Srinagar becomes oppressive, is removed to Gulmarg. A strange thing surely : there are people who leave the Punjab to enjoy the paradisaic cool and shade of Sringar and yet people here have to seek their paradise elsewhere. It is too hot for them here !

It was the 6th of June. I had returned from a stroll at 11 in the evening and had just betaken myself to bed and was about to enter on the " Midsummer night's dream" when something occurred to interrupt my reveries. Horrible shouths of "fire, fire." Like London, Cashmere is semetimes devastated by a fire which involves immense loss of life and property. The fire was raging near *Sher Guḍḍi*; hundreds of houses lay in ashes ; thousands of families had become desolate and homeless in a moment. The men of the army displayed exemplary bravery in the work of rescue and of putting down fire. Srinager officials took also a very active part in this work. But the devil too was on the alert, his votaries were no less hard-working, their energies were employed on the opposite side. Apparently they co-operated with the rescuers in saving property from destruction. While people were running to and fro to save dear life, those concealing their designs by pretending to rescue, were busily engaged in removing valuable property such as jewellery, boxes of valuable clothes and copper and brass vessels. Of these thieves some were caught red-handed, and received due wages then and there ; and people were astonished to discover among them some of the protectors of life and property, the soldiers from the army !

There is much to help on a calamity like fire in Cashmere. All the old fashioned houses are constructed of wood planks from top to bottom. The walls are of wood and roofs and floors as well. Then, as a general rule, almost every one in Cashmere is expected to have a *kangri*, a small vessel of mud in which fire is kept to warm oneself, for in very cold weather the Cashmiri goes to sleep with it. Thus the danger of fire is always imminent. People have now begun to learn the use and value of brick houses, and newly built houses are of different style.

In the morning, in that desolate town there was "weeping and great mourning.' All around was one continuous heap of ashes, reminding one of the melancholy scene on a Hindu cremation ground ; no trace of human habitation was left, except, here and there, a half burned wooden block that had formerly served for an upright. Some sheltered themselves from the oppressive heat of a June sun under umbrellas, others had not even this relief. They had to groan under the burden of this calamity—one gave vent to his grief in an "oh! the house was worth so much," another "I have lost my all," the third wept over "the earnings of my fathers." A father was mourning over his child or showing a half burned limb or simply abusing and cursing the sham rescuer who ran away with what was spared by flames. It was a never-to-be-forgotten, extremely tragical scene, which I can vividly recall at this moment as I read my notes after twelve long years.

"One woe is past, behold there cometh yet one woe hereafter." The first destruction was by fire the other was by water. All Srinagar was flooded ; the water rose every moment. The magnificent bridge in the town was pronounced dangerous to pass. Mr. Nadarsole, the Chief Engineer, with his whole staff was bewildered to see the imminent danger to the houses on both banks of the river.

The merchants commenced emptying their shops in haste ; people in general gave up the idea of saving their houses ; officials left their office buildings ; all took shelter in the floating habitations of Cashmere, the boats. But how to procure a boat, that was the question. The boatmen, seeing their opportuuity, began to pile their profits. Only the highest bidder could secure a boat. The boatmen very properly dictated their own terms. And even when you had secured a boat, there was no rest for you : all the night you were wide awake. An uprooted tree from the jungle might suddenly come across your boat—a very common thing during floods—or even the great bridge might give way and the timber coming in collision with the boat, upset it, and prepare a watery grave for you. Many bridges between *Kohala* and Cashmere had given way. There was general consternation. Men were fighting in vain against Nature. The town was half buried under water. The pleasant lanes of the Bazar, where we had walked on foot with friends, had become rivulets and were crossed by boats.

The Jhelum was in full flood. This was the condition for four days when it began to abate to the great relief of the suffering multitude. This flood had done one service. It had washed clean away the gloomy traces of the late great fire. Such were my first unpleasant experiences in this country.

I had time now to think over my future journey. The Zugi-la (pass) was blocked. To cross it and reach Leh was the next concern. In the midle of June there was to be held he famous fair in the *Hemis* monastery. I must needs attend it and be in the bustle and rowd of Tibetan Buddhists in whom centred my chief interest. Captain Godfrey was also bound for Leh. I would arrive there a little before him. If my arrival coincided with his or if I reached after him I should not find time for aything but the medical duties for which I was sent there : he was to give me work. I had to yield to Zugi-la—it was so inhospitable and would not let me cross it, however urgent my business

It was in the morning of the 21st of June that I received two telegrams from Gonda within a space of four hours. One announced the serious illness of my son, Mahmood, and the other of his departure from this life. I felt that I must resign myself to the will of God. I had come too far to go back. I could not return even if I would. There was no substitute at hand to work for me. I had placed my hand upon the plough and was not to look back. With a heavy heart I sat down and penned some very sad lines to my bereaved wife, describing to her my situation and left her to the protection of the Fatherly Providence who is the source of all comfort and solace.

June passed lazily and it was the beginning of July. On the 2nd of July, 1894, Captain Godfrey's office was to start. I accompanied one Mohammed Husain, the clerk of the British Joint Commissioner's office at Ladakh. We reached Gandrabal by boat at noon, and from thence we took horses and reached Kangan before dusk and there spent the night. Here I found a new and useful acquaintance in the persen of a Punjabi trader whose father is one of the old Central Asian traders. Tibetan he could speak very fluently ; for years he had been in Leh ; in fact the English stores shop in Leh was his idea.

To him I mentioned my purpose and he very readily assured me that he would introduce me to certain monks who would communicate to me anything and everything they knew. He also told me that the Chief Lama at Hemis owed him a debt and because of his intimacy with him would do all I wanted for his aske. I thanked him and was exceedingly glad, and from that time we became fast friends.

On the 3rd July, I reached Gond with my new friend, Mohan Lall. There we saw a novel sight ; a Pathan was making his horses inhale the smoke from a nose bag filled with a kind of grass. On enquiry we discovered that the horses had eaten a poisonous sort of grass and were almost unconscious, and the Pathan as if on homœopathic principles was treating them this way with the same grass. We saw several corpses of horses that had died from the same cause but the treatment was not known to the owners. The local ponies know instinctively the effects of the grass and avoid it. It is only the foreign animals who unwittingly eat it.

The scenery in this valley is wonderfully pleasant and is extremely refreshing to the soul of a stranger.

On the 4th we reached Sonmarg. The scenery here is more beautiful, the whole path is strewn with wild flowers that grow upon the natural grass all around. Stately trees rise on all sides, and it is a most desirable sporting ground and is visited every year by European sportsmen. Formerly it was the summer retreat for the European residents of Cashmere, but has been relinquished of late in favour ot Gulmarg, because Sonmarg is a place infested with very poisonous snakes and adders.

On the 5th we came from Sonmarg to Baltal, a distance of nine miles. Baltal is at the foot of the Zugila pass. There is no village or any human habitation from Sonmarg to Baltal. The traveller has to bring his supplies with him from Sonmarg. The goat keepers pasture their herds, and there is plenty of milk butter; extensive woods supply quantities of fuel. At that time there were only two small cottages for the mail runners, but now, thanks to Captain Trench, there is a small but beautiful inn on the spot. The poor Pathan mentioned above had again to suffer the same misfortune ; his horses ate again the same grass, and he had to apply himself to the same medical treatment.

The changes of weather here are frequent and rapid. The sky is perfectly clear with beautiful sunshine ; not a bit of any stray cloud is visible and, in an instant, as if by magic, the whole heavenly aspect becomes cloudy and gloomy and rain falls in torrents ; in another instant you enjoy the same clear weather, as if there had been no rain or cloud This change is so freqnent that, during a space of twelve hours, we observed it five times. Besides the snakes, there are plenty of bedbugs and fleas which harm the new comer.

Here at two in the afternoon arrived a company of Baltistan people with their horses. They had come here, in compliance with the order of the Tahsildar of Iskardu, a functionary of importance, with the Thanadar, the police officer, in order to convey the luggage etc., of the Commissioner from their country into Drass.

By religion they were Shia Mohamadans. They live in the most dirty and shabby style, their heads are shaved in the middle, but on both sides the hair is allowed to grow into long locks, that remain entirely unacquainted with the comb for months. They wore a very melancholic and oppsessed appearance, and had evidently come there against their will. Some of them had come from a distance of thirty miles, some from forty and some from fifty miles. They were to carry goods from Baltal to Drass and would receive only about a rupee and a quarter, that is eighteen pence. Hard must be the lot of one who has to come from a distance of fifty miles and to be a carrier for thirty miles, and then to return home with nothing more than one rupee and a quarter after eight days' travelling. He has to support himself, the beast and the family. It is to all intents and purposes forced labour.

Early on the morning of 6th July, we were ready to pass the Zugila. It is a most difficult pass, 1,300 feet above the sea level. Dreadful was our path, covered at intervals with ice that made it slippery for the horses to pass. At places the path, on one side of which was a deep abyss and on the other overhanging cliffs, was hardly more than two feet broad. The sight of danger had rendered the moods of the passengers exceeding devout.

The Mohamadans were telling their beads; Hindus were muttering "Râm-Râm, and I was meditating on the words of the Psalter "Though I walk in the valley of the shadow of death, I will fear no evil, for Thou art with me. Thy rod and Thy staff comfort me." It took two hours to pass along this dangerous path.* When it was done, the faces again brightened.

At the end of a pass their is a heap of stones, which represents the grave of some Mohamadan saint. The Mohamadans here engaged in devotion in thanksgiving for having safely accomplished the passage.

When we reached the other side of the pass, we found the whole valley covered with snow and the melting snow had formed many channels and pools in the way which we had to ford. Thus we came to Matayan which owing to the negligence of its headman was in a most wretched condition; nothing but milk and fuel could be procured.

The temporary huts were in a most miserable state. On the 7th we reached Drass where there is a small fort garrisoned by 4 soldiers and one sergeant. I found there was a telegraph office, a post office and a police station, and when I returned, I also found there a meteorological observatory. On the 8th, we halted there as Captain Godfrey was expected from Gulmarg. On arriving, Captain Godfrey was in a hurry to reach Kargil, as on the night of the 8th, he received news that the bridge at Thusgam was in a danger, and he therefore started with all haste on the morning of the 9th and reached Kargil on horse back at 11 a. m.

We were left behind and could not accompany the Captain.

We however reached Kharboo, a pretty station between Thusgam and Chanagond. There is a garden here, in which the trees are chiefly poplar and willow, having a very thick green foliage; the ground is covered with soft green grass.

This is in truth an oasis, which nature has provided for the weary traveller as a place of refreshment with its green velvet carpet, where on to take rest. Above this garden is the village, below it, a rushing river, which as it hurries down in its impetuous passage over rocks, roars like a hungry lion.

The whole path from Drass to Kargil is dreary, there being nothing to relieve the eye of the melancholy monotony of the bare hill tops save a solitary tree, here and there, looking down on miles of undulating barrenness.

On the 10th of July, we reached Chana Gund and again started for Kargil. For four miles, the path was flooded with water from the neighbouring streams and we had to climb slippery tracks on the adjoining hills, which was risky work.

---

* Zugila is difficult to pass when coming from Cashmere. The return journey being downhill is easy. In this pass, every year, a few lives are lost, and more than a dozen beasts of burden are thrown down the precipice with all their precious freight. The safest way is to walk the whole distance; people who go mounted, do so at their imminent risk, for the animal often shies and loses its balance and both horse and rider are lost.

We reached Kargil where Captain Godfrey was waiting at 3 in the afternoon. Here I formed my first acquaintance with Lala Bishan Das,* the Tahsildar of Ishkardoo.

In Kargil I learned that the bridge we were to pass over had been entirely washed away, and the passage totally stopped. No mails could be received from Leh; owing to the rise of the river, many small bridges were swept away, and the path entirely blocked.

I stayed in Kargil for two days, the 11th and 12th of July.

Captain Godfrey and Bishan Dass went to Salskote in order to arrange for the crossing, as the mail and traffic also had been stopped. But to replace the bridge was not an easy task, as the water was rising daily.

When, on the 13th, I reached the place, I saw that whatever work was done in the day was washed away in the night. The ice melted during the day owing to the heat of the sun and augmented the force and strength of the current, so that in the morning all traces of the day's labour were erased.

Another difficulty was that the timber had to be brought from a distance of 20 or 30 miles and could not be procured just when it was wanted.

Every one bound for Leh had to stop here and so our party was daily added to. There were Colonel Ward, Captain Allen, Mr. and Mrs. Coduex with us. Similarly the party on the other side of the river consisted of several Europeans. There was no means of communication between these two parties. At last we hit upon a novel plan of correspondence. The first letter was tied to an arrow head and the arrow was shot successfully to the other side by means of a bow. This scheme was also tried by the people on the other side with success. It was then decided that both the parties should commence the work from either side. We did not stop at this. "Necessity is the mother of invention," and we set about trying to exchange mails. A reel thread was shot in the same way as the first letter to the other side of the bank, and then a fine string was passed by means of the thread and then gradually a rope strong enough to draw thick wire. This wire was doubled; the mail bag was tied to a certain point and by a careful drawing in and out of this wire by people on either

---

*He is a young Punjabi gentleman of blameless life and amiable temper. His good services, a disposition to help, intelligence and humility have endeared him to those with whom he has come in contact. The Government of India has recognised his usefulness by bestowing upon him the well deserved title of "Rai sahib" and recommending him for the Governorship of the province of Ladakh. He is descended from a noble Khattri tribe. His orefathers have ever been loyal subjects of the Cashmere state and have rendered important military services.

During the Chitral expedition, as governor of Gilgit, he rendered great services, both to the Cashmere state and to the British government, and had received in recognition of nine years' service the title of "Rai Sahib" mentioned above. I spent two years in Leh while he was governor and had the good fortune to be on very friendly terms with him. The Cashmere government should be congratulated upon possessing such a useful servant. European travellers owe him a debt of gratitude and in their books of travel have acknowledged it, especially Captain (now Major) Bower, Mr. Knight and the Earl of Dunmore.

It would be no surprise if we hear of his becoming a member of the Cashmere state council. He possesses all the natural capabilities of a ruler and would be a blessing to his people.

side, the mail bags were passed from one side to the other. There was another use we made of this wire circle ; we were well provided with food, but on the other side there were no villages and no provisions could be had, so we used to send butter, bread flour, etc., to people on the other side. It was a wretched amusement, but well worth our efforts.

One night we were alarmed by a noise on the other side and learned with great relief afterwards that they had escaped from a great danger. The Europeans on the other side were living in tents. That night a wave of ice water had unexpectedly passed over the ground, and but for their vigilance they all would have been swept down the river and lost.

Here I had plenty of time and leisure to brood over my subject of the Notovitch "find." I had an opportunity of talking with Colonel Ward, who told me that Notovitch was a Russian spy who was being dogged by the Simla detective police and was not unknown to the foreign office.

To return to the journey : after various attempts, mostly unsuccessful, on the 25th of July the bridge was declared to be in a condition fit to cross. During all this time, we were the guests of Bishan Dass, who had been sumptuously entertaining us with such edibles as the season and place could afford. We crossed the river and stayed in a village known by the name of Khalsar.

On the 26th, after travelling over a circuitous and zigzag path, at 10 a. m., we came upon the straight path. This place is only 6 miles from Kargil, but on account of various difficulties, travelled by a circuitious route accomplishing a distance of 26 miles. Starting from there we reached Lausum where we began to feel voraciously hungry.

Bishan Dass' servants procured a few utensils and cooked a meal in a homely fashion, for which our appetites gave a keen relish. It was a memorable meal. There were no spoons, forks or knives ; and we placed the bread and meat upon bare washed stones on the bank of the river, protected by the shade of the willow ; we set to work with hands and fingers, grateful to heaven for the feast. For glasses and tumblers we used the hollows of our hands, and drank freely of the river water, asking ourselves :—

" When Adam delved and Eve span,
Who was then the gentleman ?"

On the 27th we started from Lousum and before arriving at our halting place we discovered a building on the left side of the river, which Bishan Dass informed us was the Buddhist convent. It is built upon high ground over-looking the country round.

I made up my mind at once to visit the spot. I took with me Janki Nath, a compounder in the Iskardoo dispensary, as he knew the language of the people of the country, and I found myself very soon in the Mulbah* convent. The room was full of statues of all kinds. Some of them had large and well formed heads worthy of the shoulders of scholars and philosophers. I first paid my respect to the idols and

*This is the spot where Notovitch claimed to have made his discovery of the name "Isa" for the first time.

the pictures and then proceeded to my interview with the reigning genius—the lama, a grey headed person, well stricken in years, who had spent 38 years there, and had several times visited Lassa. After some preliminaries in which I was instructed by my companion, the compounder, I was well received by the Lama, who consented to gratify my curiosity by answering any question I liked to put. He read to me from some book which Janki Nath translated. Then after I had asked him several introductory questions, I said, " I admire your Buddha who is called ' Isa,' read me something from his life and teachings." " Our Buddha, Isa," he said. "Yes," said I "your Buddha, Isa, 19 centuries ago was born in Judea, travelled through India, passed through Nepal into Tibet." " Quite strange and unknown man to me, he is none of our Buddha," said he. " It is strange to me," said I, " that a lama of your position should be so ignorant of a personage in the Buddhistic Pantheon who is perfectly well known at Lassa, whose life and teaching are recorded in your language and who is held in such great esteem by your co-religionists from the Grand Lama down to the lowest monk." " I have been here in this spot for 38 years, have seen a number of convents all over the land, have gone to Lassa several times, have read and conversed so much, have seen so many learned men of our people and I have never heard of such a Buddha you describe. I disown any such name." After some other talk upon the subject, I returned disappointed. Hearing of another convent close by, I started for the place Shargod two miles away. Here too was a similar convent full of idols and pictures presided over by a Lama, who had out-lived the usual span of life. He was so old and decrepit that, out of sheer mercy, I spared him many questions and had to return disappointed to Mulbah. It was here that, for the first time, I saw Polo played by the Tibetan. The headman of this place, Wazir Sanam, is a Buddhist, and an expert in the game; here too we saw the Tibetan women's dance and the whole company was pleased with the game and dance. Captain Godfrey and Colonel Ward gave the players a handsome present.

On the 28th of July, we reached Kharboo *via* the Nomika pass, which is 13,000 feet above the sea level, but the path is good. Here I made acquaintance with another magnate, Munshee Palgais *, the treasurer of Ladak, who keeps all the Government moneys collected in the province. He is a very old servant; to him is entrusted the duty of attending upon foreigners. He had come to the Kharboo † to welcome the Commissioner on behalf of the

*All the travellers that have ever gone to Leh have visited him. He has at his house curiosities from Lassa and Tibet for sale. All the travellers that have ever mentioned anything about Tibet in their books are indebted to this Palgais. He possesses land in Leh, and is a man of substance and much respected. He has gone to Yarkand in connection with the Foreseth Mission and had rendered good service to the officers. He has a passion for hunting and some of the English officials, that have had occasion to come over here to gratify their sporting propensities have presented him with guns. Thus he is the happy possessor of about half a dozen good English-made guns and about as many revolvers.

† This was the place where my friend Bishan Dass' jurisdiction came to an end; henceforth I was to travel alone. I asked him to provide me with a guide who could understand me and could introduce me to all the convents on the way to Leh. He gave me his own servant, Har Dass, a Buddhist and an inhabitant of Leh, who spoke my language well.

governor of Leh. He is a staunch Buddhist, has visited Lassa twice and knows the Punjabi language very well.

I had to ride my own hobby and I watched for a good opportunity of catechising Munshee Palgais. I asked him whether he knew anything about "Isa;" whether he had heard of any book about his life and teaching. He said he knew nothing of the kind in connection with his religion; but that he would introduce me to the missionaries in Leh who knew a good deal about the person I was talking of; from him I learnt that the Padres used to preach every Sunday and give exhibitions with the magic lantern, and that there were Roman Catholic Padres as well, who made much use of the pictures of Isa and his mother. To my question about the Hemis convent, he frankly told me that he was a member of the very convent and kept up his connection with it, that he knew all the Lamas there and was versed in their lore. He also said in answer to a question of mine that he never heard of any book in the convent treating of the life of Isa, who is a Christian, not a Buddhist saint. From the intelligent talk of this experienced old man and from his readiness to impart any knowledge he possessed, by giving straightforward and frank answer to any questions put to him concerning religion, we may see that Buddhists are not so narrow-minded as to attempt to keep their religion secret like the Hindus, who will not allow you to enter their sacred places or touch their sacred books.

As he found me very inquisitive, he told me that since I was going to Leh in the capacity of a medical man and a government official, I should have ample opportunity of learning all these things first-hand on the spot.

On the 29th, we reached Lamayuro, the place where Notovitch pretended that he learnt for the first time the existence of the supposed book in the convent of Hemis.

I visited the convent here with Har Dass and found no less than 30 (Lamas) assembled there of the red sect, while Notovitch speaks of them as wearing yellow garments.

There were the same idolatrous signs all about but every thing here was well arranged and tidy. Har Dass told me the names of the saints as he kept on pointing out the idols, this is Tara Devi, this is Lama Sangais, this is Doorgai Lama, this is Dalboo—and so on. I observed every thing. Then I requested Har Dass to ask the chief Lama, whether there was in the convent any book about "Isa" or whether he knew anything about this name. His answer was the same, "He knows nothing." I had ample opportunity of testing the accuracy of Notovitch's statement that it was here that he had ascertained from the Lamayuro lamas the existence of the creation of his own mind, the book in question.

I returned to the adjoining inn and refreshed myself. Meanwhile Captain Allen and Colonel Ward had come here in company with Munshee Palgais and had pitched their tents.

On July 30th, we made ourselves ready for starting for the next station and, as our path led by the convent, I once again entered it in company with Har Dass. This time I saw there a very old Lama, who was not there on the previous day, and with the assistance of my companion I put my question to this old man. He said that he was a man of 83 winters; became a Lama at the early age of 11 ; since then he had been roaming throughout the land, visiting all the convents, had spent a considerable period in the convents of Gavan, Nurla, Laikir, etc., that he had been to Lassa, had seen hundreds of Lamas, but never heard the name of "Isa ;" that Isa was no Lama or Buddha or incarnation of theirs, neither was there any book of history or fiction treating of the life or works of Isa in any of the convents there or in Lassa,

He also added that he was well versed in the saint lore of their religion, and it was utterly impossible that he should be ignorant of a great Lama like Isa, if he was known to any of his brother Lamas. Saying this, with an air of devotion, he began to turn his prayer wheel, and it was time for me to bid him goodbye and proceed on my journey.

The way we had to pursue that day was rough, uneven and precipitous ; the old and well beaten path had to be given up owing to the flood having carried away the small bridges upon it. That on which we travelled was a new foot-path, temporarily made over the hills.

It was a continuous going up aud down, height and slope. The slope was especially dangerous ; at places the path was only from six inches to one foot broad ; at every step there was the risk of slipping down. In this way it took six hours to travel a distance of 8 miles, and at noon we reached Khalsi, where there is a small fort on the other side of the river which is crossed by a bridge. The fort is garrisoned by about half a dozen state soldiers with one officer.

Here is a garden where we halted and enjoyed a hearty good meal ; our pleasure being enhanced by the view around, which was delightful and refreshing. There were plenty of *khubanees* (appricots) to eat. Since leaving Drass it was the first place where we had come upon beautiful scenery ; the whole tract between being sterile and stony without any vegetation.

We could not afford to enjoy ourselves here very long, and had to start in order to reach the next station of Nurla at about 4 in the evening. Here was a convent not worth the name, containing a few requisites for worship, presided over by an old Lama who conld not give us any good information.

Captain Godfrey halted at this place on the 31st, and I had time to make excursions to several of the Lamas and their convents. The previous night Har Dass had informed me that close by was a convent, having a Lama learned in the Buddhistic lore, a man of fame, who had taken his degree at Lassa.

In the morning I visited the convent and learned that the Lamas here are very abstemious. They neither eat meat, nor drink wine or spirits. They abstain even from *chang*, and are vegetarians of the first class. The vow of celebacy is very strictly observed ; no women are allowed to enter the convent, none dare to come near its precincts. Around the convents for several miles, there is plenty of game to tempt the sportsman. But he is powerless, the Lamas would not allow him to hurt any of the beasts, which are virtually under their protection.

The ibex and the wild goats roam about and will come quite close to you. They are as tame as domestic animals. I saw very many of them grazing near the doors of the convents and was surprised to learn they were all wild; but they feel and realise the kindness and protection of the Lamas and have no fear of any strangers.

We paid our respects to the presiding Lama here and observed all sorts of idolatrous furniture and decorations. There was a remarkable statue of some unknown metal fully 9 feet high. The Lama told us, it represents one of their Lamas by which I understood the Buddha. I asked him many questions about "Isa" and his book,—he was perfectly unaware of it and assured me that there was no such thing in the Buddhistic literature. From him, and from others, as well, I learnt the importance of this person, who has established his reputation as a great theologian of Buddhism, and is well versed in their philosophy and exegetics; even the Kushuks refer to him in very important matters, not excepting the Kushuk Bakula. He is not himself a Kushuk,* but is held to be quite equal to one. This convent is known by the name of Resdong.

I left it and started with my translator, Har Dass, for Suspool. Here I met one Mustafa, a Mahomedan gentleman, who came to welcome me in his capacity as one of the Leh officials. He was very kind to me, the more so because his own brother Habib Ullah was to be my assistant. He was once deputed from Leh as far as Cashmere to attend upon Prince Galitzen and therefore entertained me with many interesting stories of the prince and his travels. The mother-tongue of Mustafa is Tibetan; he knows Persian and Turkish well, and speaks Urdu with a mixture of Punjabi. I asked him "Well, friend, have you heard of the Tibetan version of the life of Jesus?" "*La haula wala quwwat*" (an Arabic exclamation of indignation), he said, "'Isa Aliah Asallam,' among the infidels! A wise man like yourself should seek him there last of all. Be sorry for your guess. I have lived among these people for 32 years, and I have heard for the first time from your mouth that 'Isa Aliah Asallam' was among the Tibetan or Hindu infidels."

I told him it was not my suggestion. I only repeated what was suggested by a European of note, who said that he had discovered a Tibetan version of the life of Christ.

---

*It is alleged that in fact he is a Kushuk, an incarnation, but on account of some great fault committed in a previous state of existence, he was prevented from assuming the title. With respect to learning and sanctity he holds the very first rank. It is a general rumour that there is hardly any book in any convent which has not been studied by this man. This is evidently an exaggeration, for there are files of books in each convent to digest the contents of which would require an age. But all that is meant, and it is affirmed by the Lama himself, is that he knows every thing of importance in their literature, therefore his verdict as regards the book of "Isa" was pretty absolute. He was the highest authority and if there was any one who could know anything about this book, it was this man. He is a great Tibetan lexicographer, and is a master of their sacred and profane knowledge, and I could not see a man more fitted to give information on the subject of the Tibetan religion, unless I had myself a better knowledge of Lassa than I have.

He was astonished and said that he knew far better than any other traveller. His knowledge was first hand, and that he knew Tibetan, and had been on the spot.

My friend pointed out to me a convent close by. I went there and met a very old Lama. His brows had turned grey, and he had lost all his teeth. I asked him his age. He said that he was only 64. He looked a much older man, like one of 90. I asked him how he knew he was not older than 64. H said that he was 11 when the Dogras conquered their country. He knew little of his religion. He was illiterate and proved of no use to me.

I then asked him whether there was any manuscript in this convent. He said, "None," because the Diwan, Hari Chand, had burned all the books. There is no record of this work of this Hari Chand, but it is a general rumour, that when the Maharaja of Cashmere conquered Leh, he wanted to build a shrine for a Hindu goddess, to which the Budhists objected ; whereupon the Maharaja sent his wazir Hari Chand to teach a lesson to the Tibetans, who demolished every convent on his way, burned the libraries and dislocated their sacred places.

There was a very large collection of books in the Buzgoo convent ; that too was burned ; at Leh, the shrine of the Hindu goddess raised its head over the devastated territory of the Buddhistic gods.

On the 2nd of August we left Suspool for Buzgoo, where there is a convent containing very many neglected books ; some of these I made Har Dass translate and read to me. I could not understand them as they related to worship, the ceremonies and the lives of the Lamas. But there was nothing about Isa or his work. Har Dass became a little indisposed here and was not able to accompany me ; and I wanted to go to Leh post haste.

I left him here to follow us at his convenience, and I started for Leh direct changing horses on the way. On my way I passed the Taro, Phiang, Gawan and Ispituk,* the Kushuk of which place I had met at Cashmere, and therefore I did not care to go to the convent.

During my interview with Pundit Prakash Ju, the then Governor of Ladakh, he introduced me to his two interpreters whose duty it was to translate the Tibetan for him. Their names were Chandan Munshee and Sano Munshee. Chandan was formerly a Lama but when his brother died and no one was left to manage the family property, he gave up his vows † and left the monastery.

He had been several times to Lassa. Sano too had visited Lassa. As they could speak Punjabi and Urdu, I congratulated myself on being in a position to secure their help in a matter in which I was so deeply interested.

After resting a while in my new house, I paid a visit to the Christian missionaries

* This is the place where Notovitch very unwisely broke his leg and went to Hemis. Leh was only five miles from this place. The way lies through an even plain, and one can reach it in 15 minutes on a good horse, and now I entered Leh, the place of my destination.

† A Lama can be released from his vow on a reasonable emergency.

and had a talk with them about Notovitch and his find. Mr. Shawe already had written a good deal to contradict Notovitch. He told me that Notovitch had never been in the vicinity and that he had made sure of this fact having ample opportunities of doing so.

I was not, however, content with his information. I was anxious to employ all means to obtain information first hand of the subject, for one of the first letters which I read in Leh was from one of my friends, who requested me to make all haste in writing to him full particulars of my enquiry into the matter of Notovitch's find. He was no less interested in the matter than I was.

I had reached Leh and my diary afterwards became irregular. I will narrate how I tested the truth of Notovitch's travel and followed him step by step, so as to contradict and expose him in a decisive manner.

Let me mention the fact that despite the opposition of the missionaries and the denial of Lamas as to the existence of any knowledge or book concerning Isa, I was always predisposed in Notovitch's favour, though he was open to much opposition, and therefore I wished to test the accuracy of his statements by personal investigation.

When I took charge of the Leh hospital, I was informed by the Rev. Mr. Shawe that Notovitch had in a French paper contradicted the statement made regarding him that he never visited the vicinity of Leh and that his allegation as regards his broken leg was a hoax, and he made bold to appeal to Dr. Marx who, he declared, treated him in his illness and to Suraj Bal the then Governor of Leh, in proof of this visit to Leh. I set to work upon this line, and to my great chagrin I found that Dr. Marx had died in 1889, five years before the publication of Notovitch's book.

I could not account for the reason which led my friend to reserve his name till years after his death and to omit it altogether in his first edition.

Dr. Marx could not be interrogated, but then he had left the medical records which were at this time in my hands to speak for him.

Notovitch claims to have come to Ladakh and met with the accident in October 1887. I inspected all the registers from 1885 to 1890, in-door and out-door registers, and those for major and minor operations, and went over them very carefully several times ; but alas! it was labour lost. Notovitch or his broken leg was nowhere to be found in them.

These registers contained very detailed and minute particulars. For instance, in one place I was surprised to find in Dr. Marx's hand-writing

Name of Patient.	Disease.	Treatment.
Captain Mowbray's dog	Scabies.	Sulphur ointment.

In another place I found a gentleman's horse treated with 30 grains of Tartar emetic. Was it a mere unlucky accident that Mr. Notovitch had failed to secure a place somewhere in one of these registers, if he had come under Dr. Marx's treatment?

In another place I found a gentleman's horse treated with 30 grains of Tartar emetic. Was it a mere unlucky accident that Mr. Notovitch had failed to secure a place somewhere in one of these registers, if he had come under Dr. Marx's treatment?

I ascertained further that Dr. Marx even in his private practice entered the names of patients in the registers, as the patients had to get their medicines from the general hospital.

It was evident that Notovitch failed to make good his claim to have visited Leh and broken his leg—and the testimony of Dr. Marx's registers decidedly was against him and Mr. Shawe was quite right.

My second step was to trace Notovitch up to the monastery at Hemis, and with a view to do it effectively I requested Captain Godfrey to correspond in his capacity of British Joint Commissioner with the Chief Lama at Hemis. He kindly acceded to my request and at once opened the correspondence, which was afterwards published in the "Christian" by my friend, Rev. J. Weber, the Moravian missionary at Leh. The original is still kept in the Joint Commissioner's office among the records of 1894. In this correspondence the Lamas disowned Notovitch, denied all knowledge of the book and refused the credit of having tended the broken legged foreigner.

To an ordinary seeker of truth, who thought that the burden of proving his visit to Leh and breaking his leg there lay with Notovitch, the Lama's denial was conclusive.

But our friend did not evidently care for the principle *onus probandi* and alleged in one of his letters that the Lamas, for fear of being robbed by the Europeans of their invaluable literary treasure, had concealed the fact and that the selfish missionaries might have disposed of the manuscript somehow or other.

Poor Notovitch, to what straits had he been reduced! There was no rhyme or reason in all this.

But we must give him due credit for his boldness in challenging a party of gentlemen to accompany him to Leh or even to Lassa, that he might have a chance of vindicating himself by finding out the manuscript of his "New Life of Christ." No wonder if he fails to gain the ears of the sober and the serious minded to follow him in his dream.

At this juncture a fair was to be held at Hemis, and I must needs go to it, as it was the most important fair, the one which Notovitch says he himself visited in 1887. The fair I visited was held there on the 29th and 30th of October, 1894. But here I was told that this fair is held in alternate years at Hemis and at Chimbray. These two places are situated at a distance of 7 miles from each other. The river Indus flows between them.

According to this statement there could have been no fair at Hemis in 1887. The fair must have been held at Chimbray. Which was it then, a slip of the pen or a slip of the leg?

Notovitch asserted in his book that the manuscript which he saw in the monastery was bound in two volumes and that it was a Tibetan translation of the Pali original kept in Lassa.

After I had spent two days at and in the fair, I went to inspect the library in the monastery, and was at once struck by the fact that amongst a heap of over 3,000 books not a single one was bound in any sense of the word.

All manuscripts are kept in separate loose leaves one upon another between a pair of wooden slates, wrapped in cotton or, in the case of costly volumes, in silken napkinsr. Notovitch's two bound volumes must have been a strange set in the land. Here was food for reflection!

While I was thus occupied, Professor Douglas of the Agra Government College came to Leh during the second half of May, 1895. He came with the purpose of ascertaining the truth or otherwise of Notovitch's allegation. I met him and related to him the results of my own enquiries. He, however, went to Hemis and saw the Lamas in person, and interrogated them with the aid of Jouldan, the Tibetan native Christian there, the late postmaster of Leh. Professor Douglas returned with his portfolio full of papers containing the questions and answers in the original language, which the Professor was proposing to send to Professor Max Müller, and was going himself to write an article, the results of his investigation.

The Professor's experiences in Hemis were similar to my own, and the interviews with the Lamas did not yield a different result.

At this time fortunately I secured a copy of the English translation of Notovitch's book, which he pronounced very correct and a distinct improvement upon the earlier edition i.e., the edition of 1894.

While I was brooding over what I had accomplished, there arrived in Leh a remarkable Lama in August, 1895, from Lassa.

He was a Kushuk of the first rank who ruled over a monastery in Lassa and had 5,500 monks in his convent under his authority. His name was Lubzeng Namhgail. He came to Leh on an episcopal visit to the Gowan monastery which is in his diocese, for he rules over a number of monasteries both in Lassa and in Leh. Here he put up with the local Kushuk, and I took the opportunity to pay him a visit in the hope of obtaining from him some information that would throw light upon the subject.

I gathered from him a great deal of information, but found him perfectly ignorant of either "Isa" or of the book on His life.

Sufficient to say that the Tibetan Buddhists have never dreamt of any such thing It was reserved for Notovitch, who, with remarkable generosity, wants to father his dream upon the poor and ignorant Lamas.

At this stage I was interrupted by a telegram from my wife informing me that she was seriously ill and wanted to see me without delay. She had been hovering between life and death. I, therefore, at once procured 40 days' leave and set out on my journey post haste.

Leaving Leh on the 1st of September, 1895, I reached Cashmere on the 4th of September, thus traversing a journey of seventeen days in only four upon horse-back, my servant accompanying me on a pony.

I was so exhausted by this long journey that I had to stop in Cashmere for a few days and saw my friend Bakula, who was still here. He complained much of the heat in Srinagar, and in proof pointed out to me his dog, whose shaggy hair had fallen off.

I left Srinagar with haste, and after various experiences, I reached Zafarwal in Sialkot, Punjab, where my wife lay on what proved to be her death-bed. Here I spent a month with my wife, attended upon her continually, and on the 14th of October, 1895, she breathed her last, at day dawn.

I performed the last ceremonies and, with a heavy heart, was again ready to return to Leh.

Now I had a girl of six years to take care of, as I had placed her in the Lady Dufferin Christian High School at Lahore under the care of my relations who worked in the school.

While I was in Zafarwal I received a letter from Munshee Palgais to say that the Kushuk from Lassa wanted me to bring him a pair of field glasses and an air-bed.

I at once sent an order to Treacher and Co., Bombay, for the articles, and hoped that the presents would go to cement my friendship with his holiness and increase my chances of discovering the key to Notovitch's secrets.

By the time I was ready to leave for Leh, I heard that my friend Bishan Dass was transferrd from Gilgit to Leh as Governor. This was an additional opportunity for he was to help me as best as he could. Now I returned and on my way I met Bishan dass in Kargil. He had come there to distribute compensation to the Baltistan owners of the animals that had died during the Chitral expedition.

From Kargil to Leh I journeyed with Bishan Dass and companionship made the burden of the journey light.

I reached Leh on the 17th of November, and then I saw the Kushuk who was very much pleased with the field glasses and the air-bed. I presented him also with a few more things, such as an English-made knife containing useful blades serving as scissors, spoon, fork, cork screw, etc., with a few oil colour Roman Catholic religious pictures,* all of which he accepted with many thanks, and evidently appreciated.

I asked the Kushuk how he knew of the existence of air-beds. He said that one of the Lama had brought one from Darjeeling and he liked it.

---

* With regard to the paintings I have my own fear, lest some one should see them and report that besides the life of Christ the Buddists keep in their places paintings of the Blessed Virgin and the Holy Child. I, therefore, make the fact public, let no one cite this existence of the painting, as evidence of Notovitch's find.

Later on I read to this Kushuk, some from Notovitch's book ; he laughed at the idea and was perfectly ignorant of Christ, Moses, Pharoah and Israel which are so often mentioned in Notovitch's Life of Christ.

In Leh the Kushuk was to perform a religious ceremony which is very similar to the Christian Sacrament as celebrated with the Catholic ritual.

The Kushuk was decked in his finest vestments. He wore a loose and flowing garment of some very costly yellow silk, and his mitre was glittering with precious pearls. This garment had fallen, as the tradition would have it, over the shoulders of no less than 13 preceding Kushuks during the scores of years before the present Kushuk came into possession of it, and was deemed most sacred and was indispensable to the performance of the sacramental ceremony.

There were today in front of the Bhuddistic alter no less than 3,000 communicants.

This was a common feast given by the Kushuk to all the Buddhists round about Leh.

There was a large jug full of some sacred element in the form of juice which the Kushuk poured into the palms of the devotees who were sitting bare-headed. They swallowed it at once with a sip and crossed both hands over the head in order to rub off what moisture remained there.

The other Lama had a dish full of large globules made of flour and butter ; they were of a rose colour. Each devotee after partaking of the 'Juice received two globules to eat

The people were sitting in rows with folded hands. The Kushuk, as he gave the juice, touched the crown of the devotee with a peacock tail broom ; and the devotee, after receiving the sacred element, made a present to the Kushuk according to his means in shape of copper or money—the women gave rings from their fingers, some gave costly torquoise, others only a butter.

All these people received from the Kushuk pieces of yellow or red or green silk which they wore round their necks as charms and amulets.

Now when I was in the full enjoyment of Kushuk Lubzeng Namhgail's confidence, I disclosed to him my earnest desire to see Lassa and accompany him.

I promised to give him Rs. 5,000 if he would take me with him and procure a safe return for me either to Leh or to Darjeeling. The Kushuk laughed at my offer and said that as a friend he would have no personal objection to my accompanying him; but then, he said, it was very dangerous for me and more so for him, for, as he said, when I had been sent back his own life would be in danger, as it is strictly forbidden to take any non-Buddhist foreigner into the sacred city.

Later on I came to know that the Kushuk feared disclosure by a man close at hand He was his personal secretary, who accompanied him always. He was a sort of spy or detective sent with the Kuhsuk to watch his proceedings and make private reports of his interviews, etc.

This man was very cunning and very exact in observing instructions from the Grand Lama.

Twice Mr. Ribback, the Moravian missionary, and I wanted to take a photograph of the Kushuk who was a fine specimen of health with a robust constitution and fair features. The secretary watched us and every time we adjusted our camera to take his photo while he was performing the Sacramental ceremony, he came persistently between us and the Kushuk so as to entirely screen him.

We were disappointed but could not help it.

I asked the Kushuk what the Grand Lama's reason for so strictly excluding foreigners from their city was. He said that the judicial authority was vested in the Kalouns, the ministers of the land who ruled the country and that it was their sure belief that, as soon as the foreigners enter Lassa, they would lose their power, and famine and pestilence would follow. People would abandon their religion, relinquish their social customs and give up Buddhism, and that this belief was based upon a prophecy of the Grand Lama which he had uttered in one of his former existences.

He told me that the Europeans were strictly watched and not allowed to enter the territory of the Grand Lama, and he was strictly forbidden to have any interview with a European.

He said that the Lassa people had an idea that the Raja of Leh (who has been deposed and now receives a pension from the Cashmere Government) was still in power and ruled the province on behalf of the Grand Lama acknowledging his suzerainty by the Raja of Cashmere, that under this belief the authority of the Raja was acknowledged in Lassa and that every year he received a payment from the people and was supported by the monastery.

And he said that he was surprised to see that the Buddhist Raja in Leh was deposed.

Captain Trench sought an interview with this Kushuk in order to ascertain certain matters connected with Dr. Waddell's researches. The Kushuk declined to see him, for he was not to see any European. Captain Trench took offence at what he thought a slight to himself. He remonstrated with the Kushuk, and wrote to him that as he was a representative of Her Majesty, in declining to pay him his respects, he offered in his person a slight to the Queen.

This communication came to the Kushuk through Munshee Palgais with whom he was at this time lodging ; it was translated for the Kushuk into Tibetan.

Strange to say the Kushuk was very much pleased with it, and said that he was grateful to the Captain for furnishing him with such an unequivocal testimonial as regards his conduct towards the foreigners ; that he would show it to the Grand Lama in proof of his minute fidelity to the instructions of the Grand Lama to have nothing to do with the Europeans.

In March, 1896, the Kushuk began to make preparations to leave for Lassa although he was to stay in Leh till June.

I asked him why he was going so soon. He said that he had received news from Lassa that some Europeans wanted to go to Lassa via Leh, and that the sacred city was to be invaded by the English army from the direction of Sikkim and Darjeeling; that the Lamas were preparing for a great war to save the city; and that they determined to die to a man before the country fell into the hands of the enemy.

I was struck by this strange news, and afterwards found out that a mole hill had been made into a mountain by the power of the Tibetan imagination.

Captains Welby and Malcolm were intending to go to China via Leh, and the settlement of Sikkim boundary was just under consideration at the time. It is evident from this that the Lassa Government has in its service some very alert detectives on the frontiers who collect every little scrap of information and send to warn the people in time.

The Kushuk left however for Lassa, and after staying one day at Hemis, while he was going to Tanchi through the Changla Pass, a misfortune befell him.

He lost his yellow gown and mitre which were the emblems of his spiritual power. It was reported to the Governor of Leh, Lala Bishan Dass, and a very thorough investigation was commenced.

The monastery of Hemis was suspected of the theft, but our Kushuk, as if by some occult knowledge, named a particular man, Raftan by name, as the thief. In vain did they for a long time try to persuade him to give up the stolen articles; but he denied all knowledge of the theft. It is a rare occurrence for a thief in Tibet when caught to deny the guilt or to refuse to return the thing if he has it in his possession.

The Kushuk now proclaimed that, if he did not get back his gown and mitre, he must needs commit suicide, as without them he dared not show his face before the Grand Lama, otherwise he would be put there to a cruel death. The secretary of the Kushuk was no less confounded, as it was from his custody that the things were stolen.

At last Raftan confessed and restored the gown and mitre and declared that his object had been to draw down blessings of heaven on his household by keeping the sacred property under his roof.

On the recovery of the gown and mitre the Kushuk and the secretary were extremely pleased, and rewarded those who had endeavoured to find them. The mitre was a very costly thing, and it was overlaid with large pearls to the value of some Rs. 25,000.

When the Kushuk reached Lassa he sent me from there a silken shawl and a number of Lassa curiosities which are still among my valuable collections.

In June. 1896, there was a great disturbance among the Lamas of the Hemis monastery. All of them were opposed to the Chogzote, the superior of the monastery. The Chogzote was accused of having disposed of a very old and valuable book that had been in the keeping of the monastery for several generations, and it was suspected that it was then in the hands of the superior of the Rezdung monastery.

Here was food for reflection. I began to think what book it was. It was said that it was written in gold and silver letters. Might it not be Notovitch's manuscript? But the mystery was soon unravelled.

The book was soon discovered, it had been hidden, by some of the Lamas in the Hemis monastery simply to give them an opportunity of accusing the Chogzote,* who had made himself unpopular with the Lamas.

I am sure I have dealt considerably with Notovitch's travels in my journal, extracts from which I have given in the preceding pages. There yet remained certain points of general interest which call for further remarks, and I therefore take the opportunity of making a few separate notes upon some of Mr. Notovitch's assertions which go a great way to develop his theory of the "Unknown Life of Christ."

* The Chogzote was very strict in observing the rules of his order and wished to make others conform to them. He has very much improved the monastery buildings and has made a very nice garden in front, which looks like some very decent square in London. In summer this garden becomes a paradise in that region.

CHAPTER II.

MR. NOTOVITCH AND HIS FIND.

Mr. Notovitch disowned any desire to inaugurate a theological controversy and asserted "perfect good faith" p. xx. Offering very strongly "his belief in the orthodox Russian religion" p. xxx. Then his translator in order to make his patron's discovery a plausible one had appealed to several missionaries who had "*imagined* that in the ancient books of the Lamas some traces remained of the Christian religion, which, as they thought, was preached there in the time of the Apostles" p. xv. Inquiries will take these conjectures in a critica enquiry for what they are worth, but they will be astounded to learn at Notovitch's feet that St. Bartholomew, St. Thomas, St. Matthias, proposed (oh! tell us where?) to preach the glad tidings to the people of the Indus, of Tibet, of China," p. xxxviii. And it would add little to their convictions when they were assured by him that "the Vatican library which is not inaccessible to the man of letters" possessed sixty-three complete or incomplete manuscripts in various Oriental languages, referring to this matter. Verily his suspicion must have been quite ungovernable when he came to know that the informant of Notovitch was some "Cardinal of the Roman church" whose name he would not disclose, even on the remonstrance of Professor Max Müller, which he resents in the teeth of all propriety by "invoking the imperious laws of propriety."

Perhaps Mr. Notovitch credited us with an amount of credulity which we were quite incapable of.

His Russian or Greek church orthodoxy looked, however, very etherial and rather microscopic when he called in question "the account of the evangelists" p. 208, or accused them of "ignorance or negligence" p. 215, or spoke of "conformity with the laws of nature" as regards the birth of the Saviour or when he frankly proposed to "give little credence to them" p. 246, or when he disbelieved in the risen Lord and discredited "the legend of the resurrection" pp. 248-9.

I think Mr. Notovitch was entitled to more credit for his rationalism than he was prepared out of mere modesty to claim.

If Mr. Notovitch came before the public as an avowed Theosophist seeking all wisdom in the Orient, we should be better prepared to believe in his "perfect good faith" and he would have little reason to complain of our "impugning his honour as a writer:" p. xx.

He gave however an interpretation, to the "gap in the traditions of the Evangelists who gave us only the barest details about the infancy, youth, education of Jesus" p. 215, very favourable to the matter of his find; and challenged us with great boldness "to show him any passage that will even approximately establish as a fact that Christ never did go either to Tibet or to India " and he promised " to lay down his arms." p. xxxiii.

What, are we to produce this evidence of the negative sort, or else be styled " the most obstinate sectarians." ?

The unknown life (Chapter iv., verse 12) made Isa leave " the parental house in secret when he had attained the age of thirteen years." Whereas St. Luke made him about this period of life return from Jerusalem to Nazareth, and live under the parental roof, and tells us that he " was subject unto the parents" St. Luke ii. 51, and here in his native country he further informs that " Jesus increased in wisdom and stature (age) and in favour with God and man."

If our Lord forthwith slipped away from paternal care there was no time left for Him to be " subject unto them " and there was no opportunity for His countrymen to mark and watch the increase of wisdom and the increase of stature and age, all of which implies an evident sojourn in the country under the eyes of men whose favour He gained as the Son of God.

These bare details about the infancy, youth and education of Jesus are replete with significance and speak volumes for our contention that our Lord did not leave the soil of Judæa any time after this period.

Anyhow this was the impression, rather the testimony, of the contemporaries of the Saviour, and our Saviour also implies in His discourse that He always lived with the people.

If our Lord has spent His youth, the most important period of His eventful life in a foreign country beyond the ken of His countrymen's eyes there would have been no occasion for them to be astonished at His teaching and asserting " Is not this the carpenter's son? Is not his mother called Mary and his brothers James and Joses and Simon and Judas and his sisters, are they not all with us—whence then has this man all these things ?"

And certainly a half-foreigner who just returned to his country after some 15 years when he is forgotten, would only with bad grace say " A prophet is not without honour save in his own country and in his own house." The land of Judæa might be called His country, as an Israelite, but not Galilee where He spent a decade of His infancy and had spent about twice the number of years in India and China.

There is a very significant phrase " He shall be called a Nazarene " (Matt. ii. 23 the import of which can be fully realised by an Asiatic only. " He is called Jesus of Nazareth " (John. i. 45) and on this very ground His claims are often doubted. " Can any good thing come out of Nazareth ?" Readers may have heard of the Persian Poet Firdausi Tusi (of Tus a town) and also of another and better known Persian poet, Sadi Shirazi (of Shiraz.)

In Asia great people are distinguished by the name of the country where they have lived, being suffixed to their name.

Sometimes their proper name is wholly omitted as in the case of Razi (Fakhuruddin, the famous commentator on the Koran), a resident of the village Ray.

Shahrastani (Abdul Karim), the great Arabic writer upon the non-Moslim religion, was called after his residence.

How was Christ called a Nazarene (Nasri) if he spent the chief period of His life elsewhere ?

Nobody cares for the children however precious—when they come of age, then only their existence and their residence is marked and they acquire repute.

The bare fact that our Lord was always called " Nazarene " after Nazareth is sufficient to show that He actually spent the chief portion of His life in Nazareth and nowhere else. Hence it is that people were perfectly familiar with our Lord as a resident of Nazareth, the son of a local carpenter and might well marvel at the supernatural wisdom which distinguished Him from His cousins though He lived with them and under the same circumstances. Hence this familiarity which begets contempt makes our Lord assert the truth of the adage " A prophet is not without honour save in his own country and in his own house."

The burden of proof, that our Lord ever left Judæa, and that for 15 years, is upon the shoulders of those who assert it, and we have shown evident reason against the idea that the gospel narrative is not inconsistent with any Tibetan sojourn of the Master.

EASTERN DIPLOMACY.

To the question, why do the Lamas of Hemis refuse to answer in the affirmative the questions which have been put to them as to the manuscript, Mr. Notovitch replied, " Because orientals are in the habit of looking upon Europeans as robbers,, and he attributed his marvellous success in getting at his treasure to the eastern diplomacy which he had learnt in his travels.—p. xxii.

It is a patent fact that Mr. Notovitch always had about him enough of Europeanism to make the natives suspect, as they do especially when foreign visitors cannot satisfactorily explain the aims and objects of their transient stay among them. After all, he professes only to have "learnt in his travels " the art of diplomacy to which as an oriental I was born. I mingled with them as a man of business, as a Government official, like many of the natives. I spent four years among them, had little of Western manners about me to make them suspect me. I won the confidence of the Clergy and Laity there and felt quite at home, was invited to their religious meetings at the monasteries, took part in their social gatherings, clad like them, and travelled in the midst of them as any other Tibetan.

Who else could find better opportunity than myself of getting the correct information on this most important matter. I pronounce—with all the advantages of collecting information that I had—that throughout my minute observation during 4 years, I never found even as much as a hint of what Mr. Notovitch affirmed and it does not contribute to his credit when he offers " to return to Tibet in company of recognised orientalists to verify the authenticity of these passages on the spot." I doubt whether there is in Europe or even in America, any company of such men who would like to be thus led by Notovitch. It is difficult for the members of this mission first to attain the standard of " Eastern diplomacy" prescribed by Notovitch and secondly withstand his ready plea of the oriental way of looking at the Europeans.

Who among the Europeans could be better equipped than Dr. Waddell ? Who entered more into the thoughts and feelings of the Tibetan Lamas than he? Who had better chances and better advantages?

I cannot help quoting here from his preface:—" On commencing my enquiry I found it necessary to learn the language, which is peculiarly difficult and known to very few Europeans. And afterwards, realizing the rigid secrecy maintained by the Lamas in regard to their seemingly chaotic rites and symbolism, I felt compelled to purchase a Lamaist temple with its fittings ; and prevailed on the officiating priests to explain to me in full detail the symbolism and the rites as they proceeded. Perceiving how much I was interested, the Lamas were so obliging as to interpret in my favour a prophetic account which existed in their scriptures regarding a Buddhist incarnation in the West. They convinced themselves that I was a reflex of the Western Buddha, Amitabha, and thus they overcame their conscientious scruples, and imparted information freely. With the knowledge thus gained, I visited other temples and monasteries, critically amplifying my information, and engaging a small staff of Lamas in the work of copying manuscripts, and searching for texts bearing upon my researches. Enjoying in these ways special facilities for penetrating the reserve of Tibetan ritual, and obtaining direct from Lhasa and Tashi-lhunpo most of the objects and explanatory material needed, I have elicited much information on Lamaist theory and practice which was altogether new." pp. viii—ix.

It is a wonder or rather pity that poor Dr. Waddell never came across the counterpart of the " Wakkha monastery " or its " Portly lama " p. 48, " who was so well versed in comparative theology and so learned in the Christian religion and its principles, who was perfectly acquainted with the Son of the one God" p. 52, and had also an eye upon the Pope the " Father of the Church."

The Buddhist of Tibet, according to the version of Notovitch's again nameless Lama, held that, " Isa is a great prophet, one of the first after the 24 Buddhas. He is greater than any one of all the Dalai Lamas, for he constitutes part of the spirituality of our Lord . . . . . His name and acts are recorded in our sacred writings . . . . We weep at the horrible sin of the pagans, who after having tortured Him, put Him to death. pp. 53, 54.

Wonder of wonders, Dr. Waddell never could get a scent of all this reverence of these pangs and these yearnings for the " Man of Sorrows ! "

Mr. Notovitch is very modest ; he disclaims fertility of imagination and does not accept the compliment of originality of thought" p. xxiv. But we cannot deny him his due ; his imagination was certainly far more fertile than he was conscious of and the fiction in the whole of "the unknown life of Jesus Christ" could well be evolved out of a tolerably fertile brain to form a very logical and systematic appendix to Madame Blavatsky's "Isis unveiled."

Mr. Notovitch, however, backed his disclaimer by a curious suggestion, "If even I have been capable of inventing a romance of this magnitude, common sense alone would point out that I should have heightened the value of such an invention by attributing my discovery to some mysterious or supernatural intervention and should have abstained from stating precisely the locality, the date and the circumstances of the discovery." p. xxv. The latter precaution, I should venture to say, he has taken to a large extent. He does not give the names of the "Portly Lama" nor of "the chief Lama" who took him and him alone into their confidence, above all foreigners ; and then he is remarkably vague as to the details of the find and his interpreters.

But as regards the former precaution it was not advisable that he should palm off his discovery upon the world in the unequivocal capacity of a Theosophist who would take lessons from the Mahatmas of Tibet who have inexhaustible store of the supernatural. Then he was well aware that believers—Christians—would give little credence to his claim and it would rather be a *prima facie* proof of his imposture—whereas the unbelievers—that is non-Christians—of Europe would reject him outright, they holding the miraculous or the supernatural at a discount.

He was very wise in adopting the plan that he did. It would give him a fair chance for issuing his book several times to gratify the curious people and ample time before his imposture was laid bare.

I fear he has been acting the Jesuit for the Theosophists.

THE GREAT MASTER RENAN.

There was a remarkable thing about the compilation of the book which struck the reader at the very outset.

Mr. Notovitch claimed to have discovered the original of his transcript about the end of 1887, but gave the result of his labours to the world 7 long years after his return to Europe *i. e.* as late as 1894. Was it to illustrate the parable of ten talents by folding his talent in the napkin and burying it deep in the earth ? He had however an excuse for the delay and I must beg him to excuse me calling it a lame excuse. He says that during the years after this discovery, he interviewed various savants of Europe and consulted them as to the mode of publishing it. At last, in Paris he saw M. Renan who advanced a very alluring and flattering proposition and asked Mr. Notovitch to entrust him with the memoirs in question with a view to his making a report on them to the academy. Mr. Notovitch evidently mistrusted the honesty of the intention of the French savant and suspected the scheme and carried away "his *work* on the pretext of further revising it."

Who in Europe has ever doubted the scrupulous honesty of Renan—who ever suspected him of adding to his laurels by depriving ambitious young men seeking notoriety of theirs ?

After the death of Renan it was perhaps the blackest calumny ever heard. Well, after the work was removed from the hand of Renan, why was it not given to the world at once—so that the matter might have been sifted at once when learned society might have been better prepared to undertake a mission "for the investigation of the manuscript on the spot." p. li, which he proposed half a decade afterwards ? The "chief Lama who informed him that there existed in the archives of Lassa very ancient records treating on the life of Jesus Christ and the nation of the west" p. xliv, was yet alive and could have been very easily interviewed. The name of the "Portly Lama" of the "Gonpa of Wakkha" p. 48, who so well versed in the mysteries of the Roman church and many of the complicated of the subjects of the Christian theology could be found out and he could have been interviewed by the "mission" he proposed—what could he gain by this injurious and unmeaning delay ?

We are at a loss to understand why he was indifferently waiting for the hand of death to remove Renan—and allow the "Gonpa of Wakkha" to change the whole aspect and to shift away the "Portly Lama."

I went after the "chief Lama" and he was nowhere ready to depose in behalf of Notovitch. The "Portly Lama" was to be found nowhere. For all these delinquencies, Mr. Notovitch had only one excuse and it sounded charitable but very disingenuous.

"Not however to hurt in any way the susceptibility of the great master (Renan) whom I deeply respected, I determined to await his demise, which sad occurrence I foresaw—judging from his enfeebled condition—could not be far off," p. L. We pity Notovitch and pity the respect which he entertained for the *great master.*

Then again with respect to the criticisms passed upon the first edition which took seven years to appear, his excuse was that of "the amount of haste" with which the book was brought out. This haste if it can be so called cannot account for what Mr. Notovitch characterises as "the inexactness of detail" p. xix.

However I have used his edition of the English translation of 1895, which he called "a book purged from all offence." I have followed Mr. Notovitch with his book in my hand and have tested his accuracy as far as was practicable and the foregoing chapters give the result of my labours which I submit to the perusal of the reader—and I need not conceal my impression that the records of Mr. Notovitch in their most essential and important position are a tissue of lies that deserve the severest censure.

It was the boldest attempt on his part to impose upon the public that always expect from a Nineteenth century traveller correct and matter of fact information.

CHAPTER III.

HISTORY.

Very little is known regarding the history of Tibet previous to the 7th century of our Era. It is just then that the mists of obscurity disperse and a glimmering of light becomes visible. Before this time the Tibetans were a race of cannibals; they indulged in a sort of devil worship, practised magic and probably offered human sacrifices to appease the wrath of the unseen powers. About 600 A. D. a monarchy ruling almost the entire land made its appearance. According to one account, an Indian prince flying from his enemies made his way into the country, Bodh-land, as the people themselves call Tibet to this day. But this is probably an invention ; it is better to believe that a local chieftain in some way or other, by warlike means or diplomacy, gained an ascendancy over the rest of the petty rulers. A great number of the tribes acknowledged him as their king, and the foundation of a monarchy was laid, which continued to exist till the 10th century. Of him we know little, beyond the fact that his rule brought prosperity to his kingdom, that he maintained communication with China, the result of which was that the science of arithmetic and of medicine, as it then existed among the Chinese, was brought into the kingdom. His son was Sron Tsan Gampo, who is better known to us and whose reign is important as being the one in which Buddhism was introduced in Tibet. At first an unbeliever in the faith of Siddharta Gautama, he was converted to the faith through the exertions of his two wives, both of whom were staunch Buddhists. Acting under their advice, he sent Thumi Sambotha to India to study the religion of Buddha and bring back copies of its sacred books. Thumi Sambotha accepted the commission with all earnestness ; he brought back with him the alphabets of northern India ; taking these for his model, he formed an alphabet known as the Tibetan alphabet. He propagated the religion of Buddha by his writings in which he was assisted by the king. In after years, with the spread of Buddhism or Lamaism, he came to be looked upon as an incarnation by the pious folk.

Sron Tsan Gampo was not only a zealous promoter of Buddhism, he was also a warrior. His frequent incursions into the west of China induced that Government to court his favour and seek an alliance by marriage, while it is even stated that he subdued the country on the other side of the Himalayas. Like his minister, Sron Tsan Gampo also obtained the honours of canonisation and was regarded as an incarnation of Buddha. His son and grandson did not possess the religious zeal of their parent, but they inherited his warlike qualities. The former adhered to his father's policy of making excursions into Chinese territory and irritated the Chinese to such an extent that they retaliated by invading the country as far as Lassa and setting fire to the regal palace ; the latter met his death while trying to quell a rebellion in Nepal.

The great grandson of Sron Tsan Gampo also interested himself in the progress of the Buddhist faith, but his reign was eclipsed in power and prosperity by his famous successor and younger son. The eldest son was one of the handsomest men of his time and his father betrothed him to a Chinese Princess well known for her accomplishments. But before she arrived at the Tibetan court the young prince died and, rather than go back, she ended by marrying the father. A son Thi Sron Detsan was the fruit of this union, the most zealous propagator of Buddhism in Tibet, in fact, the Asoka of Lamaism. At his invitation, among others, Padma Lombhara Gumpo from India arrived at the court (about 747 A. D.). The Gumpo was a professor of Magic and an exorcist coming from a famous school of philosophy in India. He did not introduce Indian Buddhism as he himself was acquainted with it, but in the system which he gave to Tibet he included a great number of the indigenous doctrines of devil worship which he found there. By admitting these beliefs to a place in his creed the spread of this type of Buddhism was rendered easy. It was he who instituted the order of Lamas and founded the first monastery of Tibet, giving to Tibetan Buddhism a form which it has retained ever since. Thi-Sron-Detsan assisted him in all his efforts and in the course of time monasteries rose over all the land. This Buddhist zealot was followed by his son who was a socialist. He was fired with the ambition of levelling all distinctions of wealth among his subjects; there were to be no rich and poor; the rich were deprived of a portion of their wealth and it was given to the poor, but in the end it was found that the people returned to their former condition. The experiment was repeated twice but twice again it failed. Of his successors there is little that would interest a general reader. After a few generations of peaceful rule dissensions arose. In 850 the country was split up by divisions, and in the course of time a great many independent kingdoms were set up. This period of strife had been preceded by a violent persecution of Buddhism, due to the anti-Buddhistic prejudices of the last king's second son.

A whole century of strife and quarrel followed, each descendant of the royal line set up a small kingdom. While all this was going on events were taking place in the west which were destined to effect the political government of the country. A revival of Buddhism had taken place chiefly through the zeal of two petty chiefs, who were also brothers, and it was a descendant of a collateral branch of the family who in the 11th century invited to his court and patronised the famous Indian Gurn Alisha. Lamaism had been steadily growing in wealth and power while the nobles and princes were engaged in fighting and were occupied too much to attend to the Lamas. Alisha's arrival took place at a time when the ground was so to say prepared for the foundation of the theocratic monarchy. He instituted a reformed order of monks who everywhere acquired influence and were patronised by the chiefs of the land. The immense popularity of this new order of men known as Kadompa, gave brith to two other sects, Sakyapa and Kagyupa. The Sakyapa sect gradually outstripped the other and when Kublai Khan ascended the throne of China he sent for the Sakya grand Lama known as

Sakya Pandita. This missionary remained at the Chinese court for twelve years and before he returned he was invested by the Emperor with sovereign power over a large tract of country and was made head of the ecclesiastical organisation of Tibet; in return for this favour he and his successors were to consecrate Chinese emperors on their succession to the throne.

But the Chinese emperors fearing that this new power might become a source of anxiety deliberately encouraged the other two sects, Attisha's reformed sect and the Kargyupa. For seventy years of rule (1270-1340), they seem to have continued in the enjoyment of their power and to have oppressed the rival sects, who continued steadily to grow in power, but the rise of the general Phagmodu changed the aspect of affairs. Lamaism as a temporal power disappeared for a time when Phagmodu after a protracted struggle succeeded with the aid of the Peking Court in setting up a dynasty which ruled in Tibet for many years. It was in 1447 somewhere in this period that the famous monastery of Toshi Lunpo was built.

The rulers of the Nung dynasty, which succeeded the Mongol dynasty in China, confirmed the successors of Phagmodu on the throne; they also recognised eight great monasteries which had by this time arisen. When the Manchu chiefs were consolidating their power in China and struggling with the last kings of the Nung dynasty, Jengir Nor, a Mongol prince, invaded the country, but he was induced to withdraw by the payment of a heavy indemnity; no sooner was this done than the Lama who had bought him off applied to the Manchu sovereign of China. This enraged the Moghuls; they invaded the country under Gushir Khan son of Jengir Nor, subdued the country and made it over to the Dalai Lama. These Lamas formerly belonged to the great monastery of Tashilunpo but through the assistance of the Mongols one of their number was elected to the Lamaship of Galdan near Lhassa. He was now made supreme in Tibet. The Chinese Governmet confirmed the Dalai Lama in his authority,—the authority which rules over Tibet to-day.

The history of Ladak requires a few words by itself. It formed part of the Tibetan monarchy until the 10th century, when it threw off allegiance to Lassa, and although recognising the authority of the Grand Lama in spiritual matters, it seldom accepted it in things political. In the 17th century, Ladak became tributary to the Mussulman power in India through its allegiance to Kashmir. When Kashmir was taken by the Sikhs, the people of Ladak threw off the sway of their masters, but in the years 1834-1841 Zorawar Singh, a lieutenant of the Kashmir state conquered and annexed the land. The Baltis were next subdued and here the progress of the Dogra empire came to an end. An attack and invasion of the North-west of Tibet was attempted but the army was destroyed through its sufferings in the snow. The Tibetans marched upon Leh, but were defeated; peace was then renewed in terms which established the *status quo* before the war.

CHAPTER IV.

GOVERNMENT.

The supreme political and religious authority is vested in the Dalai Lama or the Grand Lama. He is supposed to be an incarnation of Buddha and is elected at the age of four years. When a Dalai Lama dies his spirit is supposed to have gone into the body of a child born just about that time and a diligent search is instituted for the reincarnated spirit. They come upon a child who for one instant has the power of speech and startles the parents by saying that "the Lama has gone from Potala, and they will claim me." The gratified parents inform the priests of the wonder and forthwith the child is destined to the dignity of a Grand Lama. He remains for four years with his parents after which he is brought to the monastery and is asked to recognise certain articles used by the late Grand Lama. He is almost always successful and is duly elected to the Grand Lamaship. He is a minor till he attains the age of 18; meanwhile, a regent is chosen from one of the five monasteries of Lhassa who is also an incarnation of some deified Lama. He is elected by the Lamas; in case of an equal division, the matter is referred to the Chinese Emperor who decides which one of the two shall be regent. There are two Chinese ambassadors, called "Ambans," at the court of Lhassa; they take precedence after the Lama. These ambans are supported by an army of 1,000 soldiers; the period of office of an Amban is limited to three years.

Besides these, there are four ministers called Kalauns, members of the old royal family, elected by the Dalai Lama and the Chinese ambassadors. They are elected for life and are the real rulers of Tibet, the temporal power of the Grand Lama is in their hands, so that he is free to devote himself to pious contemplations.

These Kahlons are assisted by sixteen lesser officers; four are entrusted with the military affairs of the country, four with the civil administration; four with revenue and expenditure, and four with the administration of justice.

The four ministers appoint all the officers who are given the different districts and villages. The Lama of every village is the supreme authority in matters spiritual and religious; the *gyalpo* or king is entrusted with the administration of secular affairs. He has ministers "Kalauns" to assist him, associated with these are also a governor, "Lunpo," a commander-in-chief, "Makporn." The Chagzot is the chief revenue officer and the Shakspon is the dispenser of justice. There are besides, masters of the horse, police officers, magistrates, receiving their powers in distant parts from Lassa. If any one of these is to be removed from his office within the term, a more powerful man is appointed in his place, for the old functionary cannot be thus removed without a struggle. The new comer is expected to encounter the old official with a troop of his retainers and, only in case of victory, is to win the office, otherwise some one else more powerful is chosen. Blood may be spilt in such fights with impunity. Such high offices are, as a general rule, secured by bribery, but every officer is bound to obey in all matters the supreme authority of Lassa.

There is no regular army in Tibet. In time of danger the government calls upon every family to furnish one soldier at least. He is armed with old weapons, matchlocks, bows and arrows and has sometimes a shield to protect himself. He has to look after his own commissariat; this is generally managed for him by a member of the family who accompanies him on his march.

Armed with these primitive weapons, little did they know the strength of their enemy, Zorawar Singh, who conquered Leh between 1838-42, for his sovereign, Gulab Singh, the then Maharaja of Cashmere. The Raja of Leh, hearing of this invasion. ordered his clumsy officers to go and bring one and all of Zorawar's army, tied hand and foot before him. But one cannon ball, falling upon the Raja's palace and destroying an adjoining temple, brought him to his senses, and he understood that Zorawar was not any *gonpa* or village headman to be thus treated lightly.

Justice is administered in every village by the headman, or the *gyalpo* or the *kalon*. Curious ideas of punishment prevail in Tibet. In criminal cases, it is thought sufficient punishment if the judge hurls a series of abusive words at the person who has been found guilty, or simply to add insult to the injury spits upon his face, by way of maintaining the dignity or prestige of the bench, or the judge may direct some muscular Tibetan official to ply the accused with fisticuffs. "Benching" too is allowed by the law—and in many cases fines are imposed on offenders. When one person kills another after a brawl or fight, he is liable to be shot down with arrows, or drowned in a river with a stone tied round his neck. If murder has been committed without provocation, the dead body is tied to the murderer and corpse and man are drowned together in the river or buried together in the ground, the murderer being alive. In the case where a master beats his servant to death, the punishment is less severe, only degradation is allowed.

If a Lama commits rape on a nun, and both of them are bound by vows of celibacy, they are expelled from the orders to which they belong and are publicly denounced; if they are not so bound, they are directed to get married and are exiled from society. If either of the party is a layman or laywoman, he or she is first branded on the forehead and then expelled from society. The brand used in this punishment is made of iron and imprints the figure of a dog on the skin, so that the persons who are punished in this way are "dogs with bad names."

If the crime is adultery, and the male party is guilty, he has to give back all the dowery or marriage portion received from his wife; if the woman is guilty, he can turn her out and retain the money. In cases of theft, the thief is imprisoned, stolen property, if discovered, is returned to the owner, and the one who bought the stolen property is punished by being deprived of the stolen article as well as his money which goes to the treasury. In some cases when he has spent money obtained by selling the stolen article, he is fined and, to enable him to pay the fine, he is ordered to go a begging till he obtains the necessary amount. When the property stolen has been taken from the monasteries or the king's or governor's house, the first offence is punishable with lashes and fine. the second with the amputation of the left arm, the third with the amputation of the right and the fourth with exile or drowning. Theft in the case of foreigners is punishable only with fines.

The fines obtained from civil cases are added to the treasury; those from crimina cases are sent to the Lamas to pay for the benefit of the criminals.

The cutting of ears, either or both, as a method of criminal punishment, also obtains and another curious practice is to hang a heavy weight by a chain from the neck of a guilty man. Sometimes a convict is sewn up in the skin of an ox or cow and exposed to the sun or thrown into water. Sometimes they are branded with hot pincers. But all these cruel functions are performed by some headman of the tribe. No Lama would do it, as to shed blood or inflict an injury is against his religion. If the offender is a Lama, in civil as well as in a criminal case, he is to be tried ecclesiastically by some Lama of the monastery and leniency is always to be exercised in his favour. He is never killed; in heinous cases he is deprived of one or two of his limbs and banished, and never allowed to enter the town. By hook or by crook a Lama in very many cases manages to have the judgment in his favour.

To consider appeals for mercy, a body of men called intercessors are appointed by the government and it is their duty to plead for guilty persons who have recourse to them. If the Chief Justice or the Dalai Lama is willing to grant mercy, he makes known his decision by allowing the guilty person to visit him, this favour is tantamount to a pardon. In the meantime, while the appeal has been under consideration, the criminal as well as all relatives have been continually offering prayers for the success of the appeal. In civil cases, written testimony is always required. In cases where this is not forthcoming a sort of trial by ordeal is proposed to the litigants, a thing which they always refuse. A big cauldron containing butter is heated till the butter has melted and two stones, one white, the other black, are thrown into it. The party claiming to be right has to make good its claim by taking out with the bare hand the white stone, the hand at the same time must not be scalded; if either the black stone is taken out or the hand is scalded, the case is lost. But this method of deciding who is right and who is wrong is never parctised; it is more usual if the litigants promise to abide by it, to decide the question by means of dice. He who gets the highest number in a certain number of throws wins the case.

If, however, the quarrel still remains for some reason or other unsettled, the course adopted by both parties is to go to some monastery and hand over for its use all the disputed property.

I remember full well that a case of this nature came to my cognizance. The subject of dispute was a horse. Two persons claimed it, and were ready to support their respective claims by an almost equal amount of evidence. The case was a very complicated one; but before it came up for trial, to my great relief, the parties agreed to offer the subject of their dispute to the local monastery and the whole affair was settled amicably. This serves to explain the wealth and power of the monasteries that are the recipient of so many gifts and offerings from the people.

As a matter of fact civil cases are extremely rare; in criminal cases too no great difficulty is experienced in fixing offences on the real offenders. The Tibetans are an extremely simple people and do not conceal their thefts ; when apprehended, they take fright and make a clean breast of their crimes. Even when they are punished, they receive sentence with good grace, never failing to say *jooly* (thank you) to the judge who punishes or awards them.

A word about the postal system. Each village has to arrange for the conveying of letters to the village nearest it. Where villages are very far from one another, a postal runner has to do as much as one hundred miles before he is relieved ; he is paid very little, so that it becomes a kind of forced labour.

Revenue is paid in money or in kind or in "forced labour." People, who have not the corn, pay either in sheep-skins, in butter, grain, wood, fuel or ponies.

Forced labour presses very hardly upon the people. No time is fixed for its payment, and this it is which irritates them most. It is the heaviest economic burden lying on the shoulders of the people. Labour is exacted by the state to be utilised for public works, it is exacted by chiefs travelling from one place to another and it is exacted by monasteries.

Despite many advantages to the people under the present regime, which is an improvement upon previous rules, the people of Tibet still profess to prefer the old institutions by which they used to be governed and consider the present one an iron rule. The old rule was very lax and they enjoyed it ; for instance, if any one found some property upon the land, it was his right, the real owner was sufficiently silenced by the assertion that "I have got it upon raja's land". No wonder if they do not appreciate the Penal Code upon which so much stress is laid by the British rulers.

What makes this evil more unendurable in the sight of natives and foreigners alike is the entire freedom of monastery land from all taxes. It is no doubt owing to these severe conditions that a great deal of land is not under cultivation and as long as Tibetans believe that the existence of Lamas is more necessary than the existence of themselves, Tibet will always remain what it is, a country where the grasping Lamas exploit more and more the resources of the country for their own aggrandisement, and divert the energies of the inhabitants into unnatural channels, merely to add to their power.

CHAPTER V.

THE COUNTRY.

The table-land of Tibet is the loftiest on the face of the earth. The people who inhabit it, their manners and customs have always excited a fascinating interest whenever they have been the object of study.

This interest is no doubt heightened by the fact that access to Tibet and especially to Lhassa, the chief city, had been forbidden to foreigners. The scent of forbidden fruit is always so sweet. Tibet was an unknown country in spite of many attempts made by people to explore and describe it. Many European travellers did succeed in reaching Lhassa but almost all such successful attempts were made before the Lhassa Government acknowledged the suzerainty of China. Ever since, the greater number of persons were unsuccessful in their attempts, and if any succeeded, it was owing to the very strict disguise, under which they went; but they too were discovered by the wide awake officials who are always on the look-out for foreign intruders, and promptly deported just as they were beginning to know the city. This dislike to foreign observation and prying, which resulted in the expulsion of a traveller when he was detected trying to unravel the mysteries of Tibetan Rome, was a growth of the 19th century. Previously when once the natural and physical difficulties, presented by the mountains, had been surmounted, human prejudice opposed no obstacles to the eager traveller who desired to study the habits and customs of a hitherto unknown people.

Thus in the 14th century we find that Friar Odoric reached Lhassa, and three hundred years later Catholic missionaries visited the capital with the greatest facility. They entered the country either through Kashmir or Nepal or by way of China. But in the 19th century Manning, an Englishman, and Huc and Gobel, French missionaries who penetrated it, were compelled to return just when they were beginning to reap the fruits of their labours. Since then others have tried in the same direction—notably the Abbe Desgodins,—but have failed; nevertheless every attempt has helped to lift higher the veil which has so long concealed from our ken the land lying to the north of the Himalaya mountains.

It is not difficult to understand why strangers are thus prohibited in the country. One-sixth of the Tibetans are Lamas—or priests; the greatest part of the country's wealth is in their hands. All power in the law is wielded by them and they rule the people according to their own sweet will. They would have everything to lose if foreign ideas of government liberty and freedom were imported amongst the people. They try, therefore, to keep them out of the country especially from the town of Lhassa, and claim the authority of the Emperor of China to enforce their prohibitions. As a matter of fact they have very little respect for this great personage; in some places his rule is merely nominal and in others he is not recognised as suzerain at all.

The plateau of Tibet is supported on all its sides by some of the highest mountains in the world. To the south it has the Himalayan range, to the north the Kuen Sun Mountains. These ranges contract towards one another on the west and with the help of the Karakoram ranges lose themselves in the Pamir plateaus. On the east and south-east the mountains of China continue the elevation, forming a table-land which in one spot attains an altitude of 17,000 feet and where no spot is less than 10,000 feet above the sea level.

The length of Tibet from east to west has been computed to be over 1,500 miles, its breadth varies from 150 miles in the west to 700 in the east. The area of the country is about 800,000 square miles ; and all this space had only about 5,000,000 inhabitants.

The land could not very well bear a greater population. All travellers have only one word with which to describe the fertility of the country – barrenness. For eight months of the year, from October to April, the entire land, valley, hill and plain is under snow ; lakes and rivers are frozen and bitter winds sweep over the country. In the summer months from May to October a change commences and the contrast is seen particularly in Western Tibet. Unlike the northern section, which is a region of great plains, this portion rejoices in deep and protected vales. Here the snows melt and form sparkling streams, the woods are robed in green and nature awakes from her snowy bed. In the north, a soft down like grass springs up everywhere, making a wide green carpet sometimes plain, sometimes undulating with the slopes of hills and valleys.

Tibet makes up in its wealth of animal life what it lacks in the fertility of its soil. The grassy plains just mentioned support enormous numbers of those wild animals which are needed so much by Tibetans who are mostly either a pastoral people or are engaged in acting as carriers of trade between the emporiums of Central. Turkestan, Western China and Northern India.

Of horses and goats, wild and domestic, they have an abundance. They have also oxen, mules and sheep. But the animal peculiar to this land is the long-haired yak. Musk deer, antelopes, marmots and stags are found in good numbers. There are wild ducks and geese, snow pheasants and partridges which would interest a sportsman, but all shooting of winged animals is prohibited. Fishes are also found at a height of 15,000 feet, the close season for which is the first six months of the Tibetan year.

Of all the animals mentioned above the shawl wool goat is the chief source of revenue to the people. Its wool is the staple product of export and is largely used in making the well known shawls of Cashmere. For fuel which is a necessity in a cold country Tibetans depend upon their flocks and herds. Their droppings are collected and made into round cakes called "arghols." They are then dried and a little skill helps to make a comfortable fire. In Western Tibet a small plant known as "burtse" abounds, and is substituted for "arghols."

Tibet is also rich in minerals, notably in gold, copper and borax. The last name is an article of export ; it is obtained from lakes by natural evaporation. The salt lies in crusts on the margins of the lakes ; it is collected and purified by washing and drying in the sun. Very little gold or silver is exported, the bulk of it is used for making ornaments. There are undoubtedly many rich mines, but it is impossible to work them owing to the scarcity of water.

And another reason, perhaps, why all the possible gold is not exploited is that gold diggers are more frequently than any other class of men the victims of brigandage.

Tibet's principal import is brick-tea which it gets from China ; and one of the reasons why China wishes Tibet to be kept as much as possible to the Tibetans is that it finds there a very convenient market for this commodity. It is made out of the worst possible quality of tea-leaf, and is compressed to the purposes of export into hard masses like bricks. It is very popular with all classes and is in great demand.

The river system of Tibet calls for mention. The rivers of Northern and Central Tibet all seem to end in salt lakes which evaporate and disminish every year in size. The rivers of the south and south west flow through deep gorges, increasing in volume as they proceed in their course and empty themselves into the ocean. With respect to the entire system the whole of Northern and Central Tibet acts as a water-shed, in an easterly direction; the Hoangho, the Yangtse Kiang and the Mekong cut through China into Indo-China to join the sea, while in a westerly direction the Indus and the Sutlej breaking through the Himalayas water the plains of India.

The climate alternates between extremes of heat and cold, not only with the different seasons of the year but in summer with the time of the day. Eight months of a cold and severe winter are succeeded by four months of scorching heat. This is due to the extreme rarefication of the air which presents very little obstruction to the sun's rays. Warm days do not wane into pleasant nights ; they break off into severe freezing nights. In such a climate has the Tibetan to pass his life. He cannot emigrate, because, to do so, he must come down to the plains. So sharp is the contrast in elevation and climate between his own country and all the plains around him, that intercourse is not possible and the Tibetan on coming into lower latitudes invariably sickens and dies.

CHAPTER VI.

THE PEOPLE.

As the Tibetans are descended from the same stock as the Chinese, it is but natural that in the cast of their features they would bear a marked resemblance to the inhabitants of the celestial empire. They are a short and stunted but well-built people, adapted not only to bear the excessive rigour of the climate, but also to undertake long journeys in caravans in the interests of trade. In spite of these physical characteristics they are subject to fear and are of a very cowardly disposition. Any show of force, however slight, can easily overawe them.

Their physiognomy is by no means homogeneous. As a rule, they have small deep-set eyes overhung with a fold of skin ; high cheek bones come off into small chins thus giving their faces an oval appearance. Their noses are flat and depressed at the bridge. They wear pig-tails after the fashion of their Chinese neighbours, while moustache and beard are always scanty.

The women share all the qualities of endurance that the men possess ; in point of beauty according to Western ideas they are very defective. When one does come across a specimen with features having a tendency to please, the pleasantness is due to the combined impression made by an appearance of intelligence of good nature and calmness. In their habits the people are extremely dirty. The custom is to bathe once a year. Whether this rule is adhered to by the majority of the people is doubtful. The clothes worn next to the skin are never washed but are kept on till they fall to pieces. As little do they keep their houses clean.

It is more pleasing to turn to their character, where we notice many fine traits in the absence of which this race would only excite curiosity and not enlist much sympathy. They have been described as vindictive, but this passion is stirred up too rarely to have ever required mention. The sight of blood is enough to make them turn pale with fear. Certain it is that they are a merry hearted, cheerful people, who are never so depressed as to be unable to enjoy a joke, never so wearied that to be cheerful is an effort beyond their powers. They ask for little beyond what they need and are content with little ; the condition of their minds approximates nearest to the ideals of the poet. The vice of lying has been imputed to them by some travellers. But under the circumstances telling the truth would have placed their lives in imminent peril as the giving of true information to foreigners trying to explore the country was and is a penal offence. One rumour states that three men who had disobeyed this law were put to death by the authorities in a cruel manner. Small wonder, then, if the Tibetans, whose notions of virtue and morality are not adjusted to the same standard as those of Christian countries, should have recourse to dissimulation to save their heads. They practise in regard to strangers that morality which a spy practises in an alien country.

Quarrelling is very rare, except when they are intoxicated by chhang, and the quarrel over, no bad blood remains.

They are greedy of money—this is no doubt due to the commercial spirit which has invaded the country—but, with all their avarice, they are no strangers to alms-giving and can give liberally when occasion requires. They are also ready to admire disinterestedness and unselfishness wherever and whenever found.

In intellectual abilities, if sufficient opportunities were offered them, they would prove equal to any people in the world.

Tibet may be roughly divided into two Zones the northern and southern ; the northern Zone forms the ranging ground of the nomadic tribes, the southern Zone is inhabited by the settled people.

The nomads belong to different tribes and are known by many names, the term which embraces the greatest number of them is Champa; they wander about the extensive plain known as Changtang, hence their name. Besides these are the Kambas, so called because they come from Kham, in the south east of Tibet. Both Khambas and Champas are Buddhists (in the Tibetan sense of the word) like the rest of the people but their sons may not become Lamas. Champas do not intermarry with other tribes. Another class of these nomads are known as Dokpas, they do not wear pigtails but wear their hair long and as regards character possess more spirit and bluster than the other two tribes. A fourth class of people are the Chukpas, or brigands, who infest the plains and eke out a tolerably comfortable living by preying upon their roofless brethren. The method employed by these brigands in their attacks on nomads is very simple. The nomads live in tents and when the Chakpas come upon an unguarded tent by night, they first cut the ropes, which brings the tent down, and while the people inside attempt to escape from the folds they cut them down. All nomads carry out with them their tents wherever they go ; never accustomed to agriculture they do not care for the products of the soil and, for subsistence, they rely on the flesh and produce of their herds. They partake but sparingly of flour and dried fruits blessing them as luxuries.

There are a goodly number of half-castes in that part of the country ruled by Kashmere. They are the children of Mahomedan fathers and Tibetan mothers and are known by the name of " Argons." The male parents are traders who come to Leh to exchange or dispose of their merchandise, and while they tarry there they induce Tibetan women to adopt Islam and get married to them. These marriages under the sanction of Islam are dissolved with the departure of the merchants ; but so great is the liberty of Tibetan women—a subject of which we shall have to say a great deal later on—that nothing wrong is supposed to have been done by either of the parties when contracting these temporary alliances.

The Tibetans have castes ; but compared with what obtains in India, the restrictions mposed by caste are few. The only people who belong to the low castes are blacksmiths and musicians ; intermarriage with the higher castes is the one thing forbidden to them by social usage, otherwise there is not a shred of those ridiculous restrictions which exist in India.

The dress of the common people is simple ; it is all woollen—of a coarse, home-made cloth of bright colours. Men and women wear a wide long coat folded over double in front with a woollen scarf round the waist. The poor people wear nothing under this, and with boots and cap and in some cases an extra wrapper, their attire is complete. And the poor people, when about to sleep, put off their long coats and, spreading them upon the ground, lie upon them with their faces down and knees contracted to the chest—the cause of their crooked backs and chest—, and then wrap the part of the coat over them. They use furs under their garments; the usual fur is that of goat and sheep; the hairy side is worn next to the body. But since Leh has become the centre of commerce of Central Asia, Lassa and India, the rich men, including the Lamas and the Kushuks, use English manufactured cotton cloths, China silks and Lassa fine wools. The caps are usually lined within black fur. They also wear a curious sort of boot made of stiff paper manufactured at Lassa. To the Tibetan his boots are a matter of great importance, the stony and rough ground and in winter the biting snow require precautions. The sole of the boot is made of a piece of thick leather which is moulded up to the sides; above this is sewn a piece of felt or thick woollen cloth so as to cover the ankles; the leg is further protected by felt printed gaiters secured by a tape wound many times round.

In Lassa and Southern Tibet instead of woollen stuffs, silks are coming much into use, while English and foreign made cotton and woollen goods are supplanting home-made coarse stuffs. The dress of the Champas is almost the same as that of the inhabitants of lower Tibet, only that some of them wear the long wide coat of lamb-skin instead of woollen cloth. They have not as a rule any covering for the head.

The head-dress of the women of Southern Tibet has attracted the attention of foreigners on account of its novelty; it attracts also the attention of the natives themselves, as it is a measure of the wealth of the wearer. It consists of a fish-shaped peace of felt reaching from the forehead to the middle of the back, ornamented with stones and rough turquoises, the latter sometimes varying in value from a shilling to a pound each. From that part of this felt which is near temples, project on both side, semi-circular lappêts of cloth, edged with fur; they pass from under the hair and cover the ears.

The head-dress is called *peyrák*. All the wealth of a woman is spent in enriching it and a Tibetan can at a glance estimate the riches of a woman from the costliness of the *peyrak* she wears.

The dwellings of the settled people in Tibet are humble in appearance, they are little better than huts of mud and stone or sun-dried bricks or even of horns: a novel feature in this country. In some places they have excavated caves for dwelling in and deem them to be safer than tents. For when attacked by robbers they can defend themselves with more ease. In the larger towns better houses or residences are being constructed. No provision is, however, made for ventilation, and the rules of cleanliness are as little attended to as possible. The latrines are inside the house and are cleaned once a year; both animals and men congregate together. Every house, except the poorest, has its reception room for visitors which is kept clean, but throughout the rest of the house dirt and filth are allowed to accumulate. The oratory is also a very general feature of well-to-do houses. Whether the inmates be rich or poor no provision is made for ventilation.

More pretentious houses are crowned with balconies, where friends are received and tea and chhang freely indulged in. And a very common practice all over the land is for animals, goats, and sheep and men to congregate together in one large room.

CHAPTER VII.

OCCUPATION.

The Tibetans are chiefly a pastoral and agricultural people. The stretch of plain to the north of Changtang supports immense herds of wild animals. Here the nomad loves to wander from place to place driving his goats and sheep before him and living on the milk and flesh they yield. Whenever in his wanderings he can assist a trader in transporting goods from one part of the country to another, he does it gladly and is able to provide better fare for himself and his children. In the West, agriculture is the pursuit of the majority of the people. They form a peasantry cultivating their own lands and, assisted by miscellaneous sources of income, they manage to pay the taxes imposed on them and get a fair living. The grain which is most widely grown is barley. This serves them not only as their staple food but they extract from it a kind of beer called *chhang*. The barley is slightly boiled in a pitcher and then put aside for a week. The fermentation is complete by this time; and, strange though it may seem, in winter as well as summer it takes the same time to ferment; the liquid is then drawn off ready for use. The barley used in making this liquor is not thrown away unless the people are very rich; as a rule, it is dried, roasted and pounded into a fine flour. This flour forms their usual meal; it is not cooked up with anything; poor people take it with chhang; the rich take it with butter and sugar. A little wheat is sown and some peas. In Western Tibet, they know how to cultivate vegetables such as potatoes, onions, cabbages and pumpkins. In Leh, German vegetables have been introduced by missionaries and will doubtless spread over the whole area. The apricots which grow in Western Tibet, especially in Baltistan whence they are exported to Lhassa after being dried, are valued by the poorer classes. The pulp is often dried and then powdered and is made into a thick paste with water or tea and eaten. They yield two sorts of kernel. The sweet ones are used by rich people like ordinary almonds and, from the bitter ones, oil is extracted, which is used for lamps, and also used for food like butter by the poor people. So common is the apricot in Western Tibet that it is not a rare sight to come across some young boys who have lost their teeth by a too vigorous application of them to the sweet apricot kernels.

Tea is in great favour with all classes of people. It is consumed at home and in society. Every one has a cup made of wood about his person; this never leaves him even when asleep and whenever he calls on any friend, he brings it out and is served with tea. The tea is prepared in a curious way; the leaves are first boiled and then beaten down into a pulp-like substance, butter is then added and the whole mixture churned. Finally milk, salt and soda are added and the tea is ready. The implements of husbandry are very primitive, almost such as must have been used in Adam's time. The land is ploughed in June. The ground is first watered, water being drawn off from the melting snows on the mountains by means of canals. This system of providing water often gives rise to disputes; several fields on a hill side depend on the same canal for their supply of water, and have to take their turns on certain days which have been settled from time immemorial. When, therefore, on any day the snows do not melt, and the farmer does not see his little rivulet descend, he has recourse at once to prayer without waiting for holy Lamas ; he builds an altar of sheaves and prays for heating sunshine which to him is as rain to the Indian. When the watering is done the ploughing begins, and then the manuring. This manure is human manure, and valued so high, and rightly of course, that any member of a family will by no means ease himself under the roof of another. The grain is then sown and covered and when it is ripe, is reaped by being plucked from the roots. Threshing is done in the same way as in India. All the stalks are collected together and then the Zo or Zomo—the hybrid of the Yak and cow—is made to trample down and beat out all the grain. This is chiefly done with a view to economy. What remains of the grain after all has been gathered, is sure to sprout up next year.

The agriculturists rest in the days of winter ana try to add to their scanty resources by forming caravans to carry merchandise from one place to another. Their income is scanty not only because of the heavy taxes they have to pay but also because every one who owns land is obliged to contribute a certain amount of forced labour to Government. This burden on every landowner's back has the effect of driving him away from agriculture to the occupation of carrier of merchandise : many fields which would otherwise pay if these conditions of taxation and labour did not exist are thrown out of cultivation.

The carrying is done in caravans by mules, ponies, donkeys, yak, and sheep and by men and women. So well suited by nature are these animals for the work in which they are employed that they fearlessly follow up narrow foot paths by the mountain side. Sheer cliffs ascend abruptly on one side, while on the other is a precipitous gorge, and roaring torrent. One driver is sufficient to lead a herd of quite as many as a hundred and more; as a rule there are a greater number who accompany the caravan to guard it from robbers. The driver keeps a necklace of bells tied to the neck of his own animal ; as long as the bells tinkle the caravan goes on its slow course, but, should he want to halt, he has only to stop the bells and the whole herd comes to a standstill. The caravan, which the nomads lead are made up of sheep. These can venture on paths and over heights, which other animals shrink from attempting. Caravans of yak are specially used when crossing over snow and glaciers ; the feet of these animals do not slip and it thus becomes possible to trade in winter. The chief trading centres are Lassa, Shigatse, Gardok, Rudok and Leh. Trade is carried on by means of barter, so that both buyer and seller have to bring caravans to pay one another. Trade is carried on between these four towns and the markets of Central Turkestan, Western China and Northern India.

The women are always busy, they are even more industrious than the men ; not only do they assist them in the toil of the fields and in the carrying of merchandise, but when not so employed they take pleasure in doing all those duties which become prudent housewives. Shearing and spinning are two of their delights. Dyeing too is done at home. Weaving is reserved for men but in this he has always the assistance of females. Their "machines" resemble those sometimes seen in native towns in India, where the light of civilisation has not been reflected. Almost everything is made of yak's and sheep's wool, even the ropes and bags used in carrying wares.

Education of an elementary nature is in vogue among the people. Every family must produce, at least, one Lama, who is expected to be well read according to the learnings of the Lama, and this Lama generally induces his other less favoured brethren to cultivate a taste for learning. Hence it is that every official, however, mean and low can read and write, and a foreigner is struck to find a very large proportion of these literate people among the Tibetan population. We have already said that the Lamas form one-sixth of the population; most of them are mendicant and travel from place to place, and the Tibetan population has no lack of these itinerant teachers.

The technical arts have been developed to some extent. Their skilled artisans can produce very delicate specimens of workmanship, but richness of conception is always wanting. In this respect the monasteries which possess their own carpenters and smiths, and other artisans in the persons of Lamas are further advanced, their works showing greater skill, and better taste and design.

The ordinary carpenter works with five tools, saw, plane, chisel, axe and small hammer. Most of these are only in a "primitive" state, but the articles he produces would do credit to carpenters better equipped than he is. He carves skilfully in wood the two varieties which are principally used for the purpose being pencil-cedar and willow. Stone working is a very important industry especially at Lhassa. Tea-cups, pipes, cooking utensils, and snuff boxes are carved out of stones of certain colours and varieties. These stones are so rare that a snuff box is sometimes worth as much as £10.

The smiths have been praised for their work by travellers. The blades of sabres are said to be especially well turned and other weapons have merits of their own. Iron smelting is restricted to a very few areas on account of the want of fuel; there are many ores which could be well worked if this difficulty could be got over.

The utensils of the rich are always made of copper. Tea-pots and kettles and various other articles are elaborately worked. Inkstands and pipes, too, are made of the same metal. Copper, which has been found in the beds of rivers, is used in making articles of worship, especially prayer wheels which are very common in Tibet.

Workers in the precious metals are in greater demand than any of those just mentioned. The same artisan is a silver as well as a goldsmith as in India. The people of Tibet, like the people of India, invest all their earnings in ornaments; they have a thorough dislike for anything that is counterfeit and unreal. The smiths in the monasteries far surpass lay artisans in the quality and variety of their work. Prayer wheels of silver; trumpets, engraved and embossed with gold; sceptres, censers and images are worked more elaborately and have a better finish than what is seen elsewhere.

We have said that the Tibetans are an agricultural people; as a consequence, therefore, shopkeepers among them even in the chief towns are few in number. In a way every family is its own shopkeeper, and the family is, as nearly as possible, complete in itself. It has its own stores of grain, its herd of cattle of all kinds. Weaving is done at home, though here and there a few professional weavers are found.

Money as a medium of exchange is finding its way into the country. Formerly Chinese, Nepaulese and Kashmiri coins were used ; now, however, as British coin is used in Kashmir, it is also finding its way into Tibet. They also use "Yamboo" silver in blocks ; some are rather big and are worth from £11 to £12 sterling, but they are used chiefly as a means of hoarding. Commercial transactions, as a rule, take place by barter. Balances are generally unknown ; in some places they use a beam with a scale pan suspended at one end in the ordinary way ; to the other end of it is fixed a small weight. Grain and salt are measured in wooden cups, and straw in woollen bags. Cloth is measured by the hand—the method of measuring which most naturally suggests itself to a simple and uncultivated people.

These details, though trivial, will help to convey a better idea of what the Tibetans are, than would be the case if they were not mentioned. The mind left to itself shrinks from filling in many details which would be suggested by a concise and short description. We, however, have thought it better to clothe with as much flesh as space will allow that would therwise be little better than a bony skeleton.

CHAPTER VIII

BIRTH.

The three preceding chapters have been devoted to a description of the country, the people inhabiting it and their occupations. The following chapters will be taken up with the ceremonies which attend the three great events of every man's life, birth, marriage and death, with a digression on the social position of women.

The birth of children is made an occasion for rejoicing. Exactly one month after a child is born all the relatives are assembled and a feast is given. Each guest brings a present to the mother which is to be kept as a memento of the occasion. The party sits, that is squats down to dinner which is concluded by the drinking of *chhang* their national beverage.

The etiquette of these gifts is very exacting. The gifts are of kinds varying according to the occasion of birth, marriage and death, and also at new arrivals and departures. Every gift given or accepted is minutely and correctly entered in family records. If one has received a gift in an occasion, it has to be returned in double its value to the donor on a like occasion, and this is to continue turn by turn ; but if friendly relations are to cease, an equal gift is to be returned, and if it is not returned voluntarily, it is recoverable by a civil suit !

The advent of a baby girl in a rich man's family is the occasion of more than ordinary rejoicing. In many respects Tibetan ideas and customs present a striking contrast when placed side by side with the ideas and customs of India. In this matter particularly the contrast could not be greater. Tibetan and Indian deas are diametrically opposed. The first anxiety of an Indian couple would be to have a son, the first and dearest wish of a rich Tibetan mother and father is the advent of a little daughter. She will be a source of two-fold happiness to her parents when married ; she will not be required to go to her husband's house, but on the contrary he will be required to come to her house, the house of his parents-in-law, according to the custom of the country. The terms "bride" and "bridegroom" will change places, and it is more than merely a change of name ; the person, whom we call bride, will lord it over her groom-turned-bride, who henceforth will be condemned to a life of hen-pecked misery. The second reason for rejoicing is that the family by such a union acquires a very valuable—because unremunerated even if unwilling—servant. The only stone in the world which kills two bird's effectively is the little infant girl making her appearance in a rich Tibetan family.

The women of Tibet have recourse to a peculiar expedient to preserve the lives of their infants and safeguard them against climate of such severity as that of Tibet. This is nothing less than to fill up a cloth or woollen bag with the dried droppings of goats and place the child in it. By this means the warmth of the body is very well sustained until the child is better able to stand exposure to the cold. In this cradle, which æstheticism must regard with horror, the child continues for a length of time varying from a week to a year, and, I fear, it is this untidy cradle that imparts to the Tibetan an instinctive uncleanliness throughout the after-life.

The "christening" ceremony comes off a year after the date of birth. The baby is taken before some great Lama who is asked to select a name. This he does with due solemnity and is paid for his trouble according to the means of the parents. The members of the christening party return home, and eat, drink and make merry. If the boy is to be a lama, he receives beside the name the title of *lama-kunjuk*, *i.e.*, priest-god.

Coming to the question of the social position of women the ideas prevalent here would shock the nerves of Indians. It would even be no exaggeration to say that the state of opinion prevailing in Europe is utterly at variance with what prevails here. The freedom of women is complete ; in fact it is the unfortunate male who at some future date will have to bestir himself in the matter of his rights. As matters stand at present the man manages to get through life with a great deal of authority left him. But there is nothing in the law of the land or in unwritten custom to prevent the reduction of men themselves to that position of social bondage and subjection to women which is described in England by the adjective "down-trodden"—term so frequently used in connection with descriptions setting out the social condition of women. That the social affairs may take the turn suggested is not impossible. What would they say in Europe to an abbess ruling a whole cloister full of monks.

The women of Tibet are shackled by no customs. They go about unveiled, mix freely with men, enter with them into their pursuits of business or pleasure and partake too of their toil, assisting the men in their agricultural operations.

One man one wife is not a precept of their social decalogue. All the forms of marriage co-exist; but the right thing there is polyandry. Most people act on this basis of family life and many a woman has as many as four husbands. Polyandry in Tibet is much more nearly universal than polygamy in any Mohamadan land, the reason being that polygamy is an expensive practice reserved practically for the well-to-do, while polyandry is an economical arrangement. It was certainly imposed on the people by some worldly-wise statesman on economic grounds, as the barrenness of the country, the difficulty of emigration, due to the fact that the Tibetans accustomed to high altitudes and a cold climate are not able without danger to their lives to descend to lower altitudes, made it extremely necessary that the population should be kept down. The desired object has been certainly attained ; over-population—the fruitful source of poverty, misery and crime—is a thing unknown and the people are generally well-to-do and happy.

The polyandrous domestic kingdom is set up in this style. The eldest son of the family being of a marriageable age looks about for a wife or his parents do so for him. A bride is chosen and the marriage takes place. If the young husband has a couple of brothers, they become by the very fact of the elder brother's marriage, co-husbands of the bride. In this one matter alone she has no voice ; whether she likes the younger brothers or not she has to submit to the situation and she generally does so. The eldest brother, too, cannot forbid the arrangement. It is remarkable with what calm indifference, with what stoical insensibility, husband and wife regard this strange situation. A woman cannot have more than three husbands from the same family. Sometimes the wife is not satisfied with three brother husbands and she selects a fourth from outside the family circle. But this is very rarely done.

In European and Christian countries, where monogamy is the rule, women cannot realize how polygamy is tolerated by the women of Asiatic countries and how several wives can share a common husband with evident indifference. But the fair sex of Tibet have taken revenge upon the sterner sex, in behalf of their sisters of the other countries of the world, and they have made several husbands to share a common wife, with stoic forbearance. The women of this country have assured travellers that they sincerely pity their Western sisters who are compelled to own but one husband, and cannot realize how it is possible for any woman to become rich and be well provided for without enjoying the luxury of several husbands, who all conspire to make their common wife comfortable and feel at home.

The children of this strange union are considered children of the eldest husband; they recognise all as fathers and speak of their younger and elder fathers. As might be expected very little love is lost between children on the one hand and fathers on the other.

It may be remarked *en passant* that the children have a habit, whenever they swear, of swearing by their mother's flesh *ame-she*; it is their nearest approach to anything sacred that they know.

The term *Pakpa* is usually applied to the bridegroom and corresponds to the English word as nearly as Tibetan ideas can correspond to English ideas. In this case the bride is known as *Makpa.* But if the bride be of the superior sort and has, therefore, been ushered into the world with excessive joy, as described above, such a bride claims and makes good her claim to be Pakpa. Her condition is supposed to be the *summum bonum* of married existence. She is always rich and, therefore, independent; she has not to go to her husband's house but the poor fellow has to come to hers. Naturally, therefore, the husband cannot bring his fraternal establishment to the new home. He as Makpa is the property of the wife and can be turned out at any time, though this is rarely done. When, however, a separation does take place the lady gives the ex-husband a few rupees or some presents by way of compensation. What this compensation is for it is hard to guess; it is, perhaps, to console him for a broken heart and she looks out for another and more willing slave. Verily! *Rip van Winkle* would have borne his wife's sharp tongue with more patience if he had only known a Makpa bridegroom.

A Makpa's claims are of the flimsiest nature; I would illustrate this by a fact that came to my personal knowledge. There was one *kaloun* (noble man), Nand Ram, a member of the last Prime Minister's family. He died young leaving at home a widow and a daughter, but he had also a half brother, the son of his father *kaloun*, Gobind Ram, by another mother, a lad of 11 years, who lived in Nobrah Valley, and had some right to the paternal estate and title. This poor boy was brought home and was accepted a Makpa, a future husband by his late step-brother's widow who was 25 years of age. After some time the poor Makpa lad, though having a title to the paternal estate, was unceremoniously discarded by her ladyship, the widow, and remained dispossessed till fortunately this widow and her daughter died and the Cashmere Government came to the aid of the boy.

Polygamy is also allowed, but the Tibetans are much too poor to wish to support more than one wife in a family and it is only the necessity of having children who will one day relieve them of the duty of forced labour attaching to the possession of land which induces them to take more wives. If a man is rich or if his first wife has no children, he may marry a second, and if she does not bring him children he may marry a third. So long as they are alive he cannot marry a fourth wife but if any of them should die he can make up for the loss by marrying another in her stead. If a man and his brothers have in common three wives, and they all are childless, they are not allowed to marry a fourth wife, but another husband may be called in for help and, if this plan also fails, a fifth husband may be added. Here at last the limit is reached and to perpetuate the family, recourse must be had to the artificial means of adoption, the right of choosing the adoptive child belonging to the eldest husband and the first wife.

The existence of these three institutions, side by side, effectually assists in keeping down the population to its normal condition. Over-population is not the only evil to be avoided, the opposite extreme of a diminishing population has to be guarded against. If polyandry alone were practised, the country would be speedily depleted of its numbers. When, for instance, through the operation of this cause, there are fewer men and women, they are also richer as land is now the property of fewer people, the men contract polygamous marriages and the women, wherever it is possible, marry husbands of the *Rip van Winkle* type, and the balance of population is speedily restored.

Polyandry is said to induce leprosy. Whatever reasons may be urged against the practice, this charge is certainly unfounded, for in Tibet leprosy is nearly unknown.

CHAPTER IX.

MARRIAGE.

On leaving India, the land of child marriage and enforced widowhood, and entering Tibet a feeling of temporary relief takes possession of the mind on learning that, in this land, child marriage, if possible in theory, is never adhered to in practice, and that a woman is not bound by the rules of society to wear the widow's weeds for the remaining years of her life. A girl in Tibet may be given in marriage any time after she has reached the age of ten years but the general rule among Buddhists and Arghons alike is to wait till they are at least fourteen, before they are settled in life. A young man generally gets married when he is about twenty ; the brothers, who share his wife, are aged somewhere between fourteen and eighteen.

The betrothal of man and woman is an affair in which they are allowed little, if any, voice. Anxious parents with the assistance of good old relatives of match-making celebrity arrange the affair. Beauty is considered a quality of very little value in a bride; a beautiful girl is sure to prove troublesome, so the Buddhists with sound sense put this attribute in the background. What is really more important is wealth, and if, in addition to this, a girl has the abilities necessary to manage her property successfully, it will more than compensate for any defects she may possess. When the parents of a young man have selected a bride who, from their point of view, has everything that is necessary to make a suitable wife, the Lamas are called in and consulted, who, like the Hindus in India, read their books to find out if the destinies of the two lie along the same path. If the answer is unfavourable, the match must be given up and a second shaking of heads among relatives and much anxious discussion arise which result, perhaps, in a happier choice. If the fates are favourable this time, the betrothal is sanctioned. A curious method of betrothal exists which requires to be noticed. It is fantastic in the extreme. When a male child possessing property is left alone in the world he is betrothed at once to some fully grown woman who acts as his nurse during childhood and steps into the position of wife when her charge has grown up to a marriageable age. The dowry is a question of the greatest importance to the money-loving Tibetan ; it is fixed at the time of betrothal but it is not given till the marriage takes place and sometimes the payment of it is delayed even after that occasion. The interval between betrothal and marriage or the period of courtship varies from a few weeks to a year. On the day of the betrothal the " groom " proceeds to the house of his future wife with a bowl of chhang and the people assembled there fix the wedding day. Until that day arrives it is the duty of the bridegroom to send every day to his wife-elect a share of his food and chhang. After a few days it becomes the duty of the " groom " to make a present varying in value according to his means, to the mother-in-law.

We pass on to the marriage ceremony. The procedure is curious and quaint, and a study in itself. On the appointed day at nightfall the relatives of the birdegroom assemble at his house, the bride's house being the rendezvous of the other party. A small band of five or seven, one of whom is the bridegroom sets out to make the proposal in due form, on coming to the door of the yard surrounding the house they find it guarded by male relatives of the bride who refuse to allow the bridegroom to enter. They are, however, won over by a gift of money and the ardent lover finds himself within. After entering this yard, another difficulty confronts him ; before the door of the house the ladies have posted themselves ; they pretend to be very angry at the intrusion and beat him with tiny sticks. But by nothing daunted this hero fires off his squibs in the shape of mammon's gifts and with terrible effect. Wrath is appeased and opposition laid low. He next enters the house where a different reception awaits him and his friends. The bride's party entertains them to as rich a banquet as their means can afford. Everyone is present save the bride. Chhang drinking, music, and dancing are indulged in till the small hours of the morning. Then, the best man accompanied by some of the elders proceeds to the kitchen followed by the parents and relatives of the bride. The bridegroom is not one of them. The guests sit down, each one placing his cup before him. Two of the bride's relatives, one a man the other a woman go round the seated circle ; the former fills the cups with chhang, the latter who has a stick in her hand freely uses it on any guests whose powers of drinking are defective. When this performance is over, they go to another part of the house ; here two representatives of the bride and bridegroom stand up to sing sonnets, each one singing in praise of the person represented by his opponent. These sonnets are not extempore compositions, they are taken from the marriage or bridal songs of the country of which there are a great many. Sometimes as many as forty may be sung. The first sonnet is sung in praise of the bridegroom by the representative, who is also a relative of the bride. This is replied to by a song by the other party in honour of the bride. The performance comes to an end when the memory of the one or the other fails and verses are no longer forthcoming. It is in fact an intellectual contest and the one who fails to reply to his adversary has to pay a sum of money, if he has not the money, a goat, as a fine.

The curtain now falls on this act and the scene of the next is the reception room or hall. A rope is stretched across the room and from it the parents of the bride suspend the fine clothes and ornaments, and a box containing money, which are to be given away with the bride. A list of everything given away is made out and treasured up as a memento of the grandeur of the occasion. The best man is put in possession, and then at last he thinks of remarking what is doubtless very true, that it is getting late and he would be glad if the bride were made over to him.

Here another difficulty springs up. Verily the course of true love never runs smooth. least of all in mountainous Tibet; the bride is not to be found, her young friends who dislike the idea of separation have hidden her and the relatives are unable to find out where she is hid. The old tactics are tried and found successful. The bride is brought forth but she is in a flood of tears and is led up to her mother to say farewell. She embraces her feet in token of submission evidently to her choice in regard to the bridegroom, she embraces likewise the feet of all her relatives. The best man then places a broad-brimmed hat on her head and fastens round it a symbolical scarf. This done, her uncle steps forward and carries her out on his back to a place where a horse is in waiting. A procession is now formed to the groom's house. All are mounted on horseback. The best man leads followed by the groom's party. Then comes the bridegroom, in the oriental style, after the bride—not a look or a word has passed between them to-day and the rear is brought up by the bride's friends, musicians and spectators. As the wedding party passes by houses or villages on its way to the groom's house, the villagers come out with offerings of "sattoo and butter." The best man touches these offerings in sign of acceptance and in return gives a small present to the persons bringing them.

On arriving at the bridegroom's house, the door is found open and, in front of it are some Lamas. The bridegroom and his party dismount: here at last the tongue of the unromantic youth finds utterance, but it is only to bid his bride to dismount. The answer to his request is a burst of tears which flow more copiously than ever. Nothing will induce her to come down but the sight of the *almighty dollar* or whatever Tibetans used instead. The couple stand before the Lamas with clasped hands and bowed heads while certain prayers are read. The prayer book is held by a novice of low rank, the head Lama officiates, and as he goes on reading he scatters with his right hand grains of rice and barley, while with his left he shakes a staff to which a bell is attached. The bridal party then enters the bridegroom's house where they see two mystic signs, traced by the Lamas in barley or other grain on the floor. One of these indicates the spot where the bride is to sit down and the other where the bridegroom. Between them is placed a measure full of grain; in this is stuck an arrow with a lump of clarified butter at the top. The groom's mother come up to offer chhang to the newly married pair, and, after this, a Lama sprinkles them with holy water. This completes the religious portion of the ceremony. The next item is the marriage feast. It is just as merry and jovial as any other marriage feast in the world. The only difference is that Tibetan people partake of Tibetan dishes in Tibetan style. In the evening the bride decked in her best garments wearing every jewel that she possesses, and, accompanied by her husband, exhibits herself to an admiring throng of friends and relatives. This may be regarded as a Tibetan "coming out" corresponding to the English coming out. True the Tibetan ceremony takes place after marriage, while the European ceremony takes place before, but this is in accordance with the topsy-turvydom of things. The "coming out" is followed by a dance in which men dancewith men and women withwomen again contrary to English ideas to The bride and bridegroom have to dance certain dances before they are at liberty to retire. When they have gone the merry-making goes on without them, and the party disperses the next day. On the eighth day the newly married couple visit all their relatives, after which they return home to commence their married life.

If the parents of the bride and bridegroom are too poor to bear the expenses of a regular wedding, they arrange that the bridegroom shall come quietly one night and elope with his lady-love. No civil or religious marriage ceremony is performed. They can, however, if their means allow it, give a regular marriage feast after the lapse of a year or so, but the fact of its not being given does not invalidate the marriage. It is considered the correct thing to provide a marriage feast, for the giving of it gratifies the vanity of the giver, and what is more important, if no such feast is given, the bridegroom does not receive the valuables that are always given on such an occasion.

The Tibetans in this respect entertain a very high—but very inconvenient—ideal of honour, and for the father not to be able to provide for his daughter's marriage expenses is regarded as a greatest disgrace. In November, 1895, early of a morning I was waked by my friend Bishun Das, who informed me that some one in Gunpa village had committed suicide by strangling himself—a very common form of suicide, as they cannot afford a revolver or poison. On enquiry we learnt that the unfortunate man had not the wherewithal for the marriage of his grown up daughter and could not bear the disgrace, hence the desperate deed. Several such cases came to my knowledge afterwards. A suicide, as is the case in other countries, meets with little ceremony after death.

While the marriage ceremony is so protracted in length as to require, when only half of it has been finished, a hint from the best man that matters should be gone through briskly, the formality which accompanies a divorce is simpler than one might expect it to be. The ceremony consists of nothing more than snapping a thread, the ends of which are tied to a finger of husband and wife respectfully.

The death of a husband gives a woman the right, if she chooses to exercise it, of divorcing herself from her dead husband by going through this ceremony. The younger husbands thus loose her and cannot prevent it. As a matter of fact, a woman rarely divorces herself from her dead husband when she has children, because they inherit the family property ; and the younger husbands continue in a position subordinate to that of the heirs. However, if she insists on a divorce, all children over the age of eight are to be made over to their minor father. She herself is free and is allowed by the custom of the land to remarry as often as nine times, but after the ninth remarriage she must be content to remain a widow. In case of a divorce, it is considered improper for either party to remarry within a year of the death of the deceased. The same rule is followed when a wife dies.

If a Buddhist couple cannot agree they refer their dispute to an arbitrator, who, if he thinks matters cannot be amicably arranged, decides that they must separate. Each party retains his or her own property, while no stigma attaches to either as long as "incompatibility of temper" is the ground for the separation. Children under eight remain with the mother till they arrive at that age; they are then made over to the father, whose heirs they eventually become. Except in the case of a "makpa" husband a Tibetan woman cannot divorce rhe husband against his will, but a man may divorce his wife for adultery. In such a case, circumstantial evidence for the crime is not enough, and a man who had taken proceedings against his wife unless she had been taken *in flagrante delicto* would be looked down upon. Divorces of this kind are rare, the offence is looked upon as an infringement of private rights in property rather than as anything more serious ; consequently, if the offending wife is willing to return to her husband, the latter usually consents to hush the matter up in consideration for a sum of money paid to him by the wife's lover. If the woman refuses to return to her husband, the latter can divorce her and retain possession of her property. If for any other cause, he wishes to divorce her and the younger husbands do not consent to the separation, he has to provide them with so much land as will suffice to supply their needs and enable them to set up house on their own account.

CHAPTER X

PHYSIC.

We have referred to the topsy-turveydom considered from the civilised standpoint of ideas which prevail in Tibet regarding the position of women. Another instance of this is the method of treating the sick. The Tibetan's imagination peoples the world about him with innumerable spirits, shapes, shadows, and devils, and when anyone falls sick he skillfully diagnoses the case by saying that a devil has entered the sick man. The patient's first concern, therefore, is to get rid of this devil and he runs to some wise-a-cre and gets a charm from him. This consists of a piece of paper inscribed with prayers and incantations and is hung round the neck of the sick man or it is sometimes made up into pills and swallowed. When it is found that this does not produce the desired effect, recourse is had to a neighbouring Lama and his mode of treatment is as simple as the former one. He makes a figure of clay, lights his many-flamed lamp and offers prayers that the devil may be induced to change his dwelling-place from the body of the man to the little clay figure. The figure is then burnt and the devil is supposed to be destroyed.

This remedy came to my knowledge in a curious way. My friend, Mohan Lal, whom I have mentioned already was suffering from bubo and was, as I supposed, under my medical care. One evening I heard he was very bad, so went to his place, but found to my utter astonishment, that there were in the house no less than a score of Lamas engaged in a wierd ceremony which reminded me of Macbeth's witches. There were 151 lamps burning round a mud statue of Mohan Lal's size clad in the patient's clothing—there was also incense burning and the Lamas were making a great noise, playing upon their crude instruments, and drinking tea in cups placed in rows. To my astonishment I learned that my patient was being treated with spiritual physic for the bubo he was suffering from, and Mohan Lal confessed that he had only consulted me out of respect but had never acted upon my advice or used my medicines, but had depended wholly upon the Lamas and their treatment. I also saw an amulet tied upon the part where the bubo was being developed. The treatment of the Lama was ineffectual and he was removed to Cashmere where he was out of the reach of the Lamas; there he recovered under the treatment of some quack Indian surgeon. But this too proves ineffectual, so the next remedy is to get a number of Lamas to come to the sick man's house and there offer prayers for his recovery. The Lamas are guests of the house and they stay for as many days as the means of the family will allow, the number of those who come, and the prayers they say are limited by the same considerations. And if this treatment proves to be of no avail, it is concluded that the dignity of the Lamas is not sufficient to expel the diabolical influence, and they must needs send for an abbot who comes dressed in his priestly vestments to heal the sick man. His method is very drastic; he has lamps burning like the others, but he is not content with prayers and charms; he has a sharp iron instrument for which the word stiletto would be too mild; with this he begins to screw, with some force, into the skin of the sick man's stomach bidding the devil come out. It would seem as if the command were obeyed for the unfortunate fellow is pained beyond endurance, and has no alternative but to say he feels better and that the devil is gone; but the relief is feigned and the sickness grows, and now at last he seeks a remedy in the proper direction; he goes to a physician. Could topsy-turveydom be more complete. The Tibetan consults the physician last of all, after he has tried everyone and every thing and failed. Europeans and educated Indians go to him first. One would expect that faith in the efficacy of the Lamas' prayers would be shaken by their failures, which doubtless are many. Not so; if the physician helps the sick man to recover, all the credit is claimed by the Lamas, who maintain that the recovery is due to the after effects of their prayers; but if the patient dies, Tibetan logic places the blame on the physician. Who is not less blameable than the exorcist? Physicians here form a hereditary caste; they add greatly to their professional reputation by going through a course of instruction at Lhassa. Their great panacea for all remedies is butter, internally and externally. For local diseases a piece of sheepskin is always applied; if it is earache, sheepskin will cure it; if it is toothache, sheepskin will allay it; if it is a headache, sheepskin will drive it away; so that sheepskin occupies somewhat the same place in Tibet as Beecham's pills do in India; it cures or professes to cure everything. There is, however, an exception made in favour of some seeds like those of tomato which are applied to the face in cases of facial neuralgia. They are of a bright brownish colour, and women also apply them in a way that renders their faces, according to their ideas, pretty, for they look fair and red under its effect. It takes the place of painting as practised in European countries. The doctors know something of the properties of some plants; while mixing them they recite certain formulæ. They believe in the usefulness of prescribing certain diets for certain sicknesses. Cauterisation, bleeding and dry and moist cupping comprise the entire stock of their surgical operations. In a case of sore-eyes they apply, a piece of paper used as wrapper for brick tea imported from Lassa.

The hot saline springs of Tibet which contain Borax, Sulphur, Soda and other minerals, are also used to treat disease—especially vinereal diseases which are becoming more and more common in the country. These springs flow out of rocks, and tanks are dug out to receive them. There are three tanks generally to every spring. To obtain the full benefit of the mineral waters, a diseased man must bathe in the first tank for seven days, if this does not set him up, he must bathe for a whole fortnight in the second; and if he is still unbenefited, he must try the third tank for twenty-one days. These springs have been found beneficial in cases of rheumatism and some skin disease; why it is that physicians direct their patients to bathe according to the method here described it is not easy to say; poor people, as a rule, do not stay for more than a few days at these bathing places. The science, if science it can be called, of midwifery is in the possession of the old women; there is no class of midwives there such as we have now in India, but the old women are but one degree less skilful than the unexperienced *dais*.

The crude beginnings of certain sort of veterinary knowledge are also there. Cattle are dosed in the nose; in the case of horses and bulls, the medicine is inserted in the right nostril ; in the case of mares and cows, the nostril selected is the left. Bleeding in veterinary practices is done with a long needle, which is passed through the nostrils anterior and posterior, and the palate artery is pierced through. The cure for colic is hard and swift riding, so that it no doubt pays to get colicky animals. Treatment for disease, in the case both of animals and men, must not begin on a day which they believe is unlucky.

The doctors generally carry about their stock of medicines with them going from one house to another like the old time hawkers. The fees charged seem very small if expressed in English money ; sixpence and a pot of chhaug with a piece of cloth is the usual remuneration for a fortnight's medical attendance.

The practice among nomads is to leave a sick man behind with sufficient food and water to enable him to recover by himself aided by the efforts of nature. This seems barbarous, but nomads must wander from day to day to maintain themselves ; travelling does not conduce to recovery and as a rule the invalid is left behind in a spot where other nomads are expected to camp and on whose assistance and services to the sick men they always rely and are seldom disappointed.

Tibetans do not believe in vaccination ; they have a method of preventive treatment of small-pox which suggests, but is not, inoculation. The scab of the small-pox is dried and swallowed, and this is supposed to guard a person against the fell disease. When, however, anyone is afflicted with it, whoever it may be even a dear parent, the person is removed to a deserted place and left with food and water to recover or die there ; in the case of death the body is thrown into a river.

When an epidemic breaks out they adopt a singular expedient to prevent one village from taking the infection from another. This is nothing less than to pile up thorns and thorny bushes on all paths especially those on bridges which lead from one village to the other, the rationale of these precautions is to prevent the mischief-working devils from transferring their operations from a place which is infected to one which is not.

What with their belief in the power of devils, in the power of Lamas and charms and the small fees paid by the people—Tibet does not fulfil the conditions of a Physician's utopia.

CHAPTER XI

BURIAL.

The usual method of disposing of their dead is cremation : if the death is due to smallpox, the corpse is not cremated but thrown into a river or a lake or buried. They are not anxious to get rid of the corpse as soon as possible ; they keep the body as long as they can and consider it a matter for congratulation if death occurs in winter rather than in summer. In the former case the corpse may be kept for fifteen or sixteen days before it is cremated ; during all this time Lamas are in attendance, ministering with ceremonies, and offering prayers with the object of assisting the soul in obtaining a suitable second birth. In summer all this has to be cut short, as, owing to the heat, corruption sets in sooner : the body must be cremated on the third day and the soul's chances of obtaining a suitable rebirth are seriously diminished.

Cremation is in vogue especially in the western portion of Tibet where there is no lack of fuel, but other parts have other customs as well. In central Tibet they expose the corpses upon high peaks of hills, to be eaten up by vultures &c. In Lassa they cut up the corpse into pieces and place it before the dogs, who devour it, the bones are pounded and made into balls with flour, to be eaten up by the dogs. This is a mark of distinction that does not fall to the lot of everyone. The corpses of Lamas are exposed upon hills, that they may be eaten up by birds of prey and no portion of the sacred body be allowed to fall upon unclean ground. Where fuel can be had the Lama's corpse is burned and the ashes sold to the worshippers, who set a high value upon these relics. Distinguished Lamas are buried ; the corpse is placed in a coffin along with some sacred manuscript written by the Lama himself some prayers from the same source, the cups and prayer wheel and other accessories of worship. Sometimes, corn, metal as gold, silver and copper, and also precious stones are placed in the coffin. This coffin is put in a sort of mossolium called *chhortan* ; the Grand Lama is embalmed. His face is decorated with gold and precious stones often to the value of several lakhs of rupees. When placing the corpse in a coffin they deposit these sacred treasure in a *chhortan.* It is well known that in Lassa there are many treasures under ground. No doubt every *chhortan*—and there are many if excavated—would reveal a treasure with the memory of a Delai Lama.

The relatives of the dead man assemble at the house of the deceased on the cremation day. "Chang and suttoo" are provided for all who attend. They eat and drink but sadly, their countenances are full of grief, and everyone is silent.

The abbot from the nearest monastery is next sent for. This dignitary on arriving reads certain prayers from a sacred book which he holds in one of his hands ; with the other hand he takes hold of the pig tail of the deceased, if a male ; the hair, if a female. As he goes on reading, he keeps pulling and jerking the hair of the corpse. Should any blood ooze out of the head by the time that the reading is over—it lasts about half an hour—it is considered a very auspicious sign as proving that the spirit of the deceased has entered into the presence of the divine, and has entered nirvana or become annihilated, the highest condition of future happiness according to the creed of Buddha. But if no blood be visible, the inference is that the dead person's spirit is wandering about in space, restlessly awaiting re-embodiment. It will then be the business of the Lamas, on being paid for it, to offer prayers to accelerate the desired event.

When the prayers are over the abbot stands aside, and from seven to nine of the members of the family come with ropes and tie the deceased into a squatting position; knees, hands, neck, all are tied close together; if the corpse has become stiff, the bones are broken to allow it to be fixed in the required posture. The corpse is then placed in a bag made of cotton cloth, and carried from the room in which it has been lying to the room which is set apart for family worship. Here it is placed in a corner, and a piece of cloth, or a wide shawl is stretched from one wall to the other to conceal it from view. The abbot then comes in and sits down just to the left hand side of the corpse, with his back to it; other Lamas of inferior rank come in also and sit facing the abbot. All relatives and friends now retire, leaving the priests alone with the corpse. The duty of the priests is to pray and to keep alight the 101 lamps of brass. They also offer food and drink to the deceased. They remain there watching and praying by day and by night till the hour for cremation arrives: seven to ten Lamas are present by day and one or two by night. The day for cremation is chosen by the Lamas themselves: and that which their sacred books tell them is most auspicious.

When the day arrives the heir and the next of kin of the dead man enter the room. One of them lifts the corpse and delivers it to the chief mourners, who stoop down to receive it, and with the aid of two sticks, and assisted by the others, carry it to the door of the house. A square-shaped coffin, provided by the monastery whose monks are conducting the obsequies, is brought and the corpse is placed in it. It is then borne on the shoulders of the relatives to the burning ground. If the chief mourner is a woman, she does not come to the burning ground, but, after she has walked three times round the coffin and prostrated herself before it each time she is conducted back to the house. On the way to the burning ground, the Lamas go in front praying and playing on musical instruments; then follow the friends and relatives, and last of all comes the coffin. Everyone following the body carries with him a piece of wood to the oven or furnace, where the body is to be burnt. Each family has one such furnace or oven reserved for the cremation of its dead. The wood is then piled on top of the furnace and butter is poured over the corpse. All the relations of the dead man then walk round this furnace three times, and bow down as many times at the starting point, remaining all the while bare-headed.

While the cremation is going on the Lamas continue praying in dirge-like tones; with an accompaniment of drums. When the first bone drops from the body the funeral ends, though one of the family must remain until the body is wholly consumed. The Lamas take the first bone back to the worship room of the deceased, then pound it up, mix it with a little clay and make it into a figure or idol. If the deceased was a rich man the figure is placed in a "chorten" built for the purpose; if he was a poor it is put in any other old "chorten" where other figures belonging to poor men have already been deposited. When the cremation is over, those who have remained behind to see the last of it raise the farewell shout "Have done with this world now," and run away as fast as they can. On the evening of this day an open air feast is given to the mourners. The friends of the family offer presents, a list of which is made out and carefully preserved. The party then disperses.

On the morning of the next day some one, who is interested in the matter, comes up to see if any footprints can be observed among the ashes. By this means he can inform himself of the particular kind of animal into which the soul of the dead man has entered. If the footprints are those of a crow, he knows that his friend has become a member of the winged creation. But it is believed that for a few days the soul will have no rest in its efforts to get re-embodied. So it has to wait for some time before it can join the cawing fraternity, On the day that it does so, the Lamas write a letter requesting it not to rove about and send the letter to the realms of ghosts by burning it, an act which is accompanied by ceremonies. In the home of the deceased food is placed in different places showing the earnestness of the desire of friends and relatives to assist the soul in its troubles.

Before closing the description of this last scene of human life, it is worth mentioning that the Tibetan mourner hangs a white sheet at the door of his house and puts on white garments. White is the mourning colour with these people. What a marked contrast to the European custom! To a Christian, however, this is appropriate. It reminds him of what the apostle says of "keeping oneself unspotted from the world," and it may probably be found that some such metaphorical idea has been the origin of this custom. The mourning does not last long, and the feeling "let the dead past bury its dead" brings back the old routine of life.

CHAPTER XII.

SPORTS, AMUSEMENTS AND FESTIVALS.

The people are well provided with amusements and festivals. Among the former beside Polo we note archery, in which young men attain such accuracy and skill that while going at full speed on horseback they can turn round and hit a mark they have set up. The sport is very popular: whole villages turn out to practise: they aim at targets with bull's eye centres. Archery is indulged in, to a great extent, by farmers, because it is believed to be a mode of deciding whether the coming year is to be one of prosperity or not. Before the time for ploughing has arrived, a large number of farmers turn out with bows and arrows on a day previously appointed, and shoot six arrows each at a target placed at some distance. They shoot in turn. One man may get his turn as often as three or four times. He who succeeds in shooting six arrows correctly in the course of the day is sure to have good luck that year, and for ever after. All his friends come round and congratulate him, and while this goes on a young maiden comes in front and makes a deep obeisance. In the evening all the villagers assemble at a "common room," or village assembly room, to make merry and rejoice over the event. A feast is provided for them all by contributions levied from the villagers, and thus the operations of agriculture commence.

Hunting is another recreation, as it is also a means of subsistence. To hunt the Ibex a great crowd assembles. The headmen of the villages ascertain what places are frequented by these animals. On the day previous to the hunt the heights surrounding one of these places are occupied by bodies of men provided with tom-toms, as many as two or three hundred being often told off for this purpose. Early in the morning the huntsmen with their matchlocks descend into the open space below and conceal themselves along the course which they expect the animals to try to escape when surprised. All of a sudden tom-toms begin to fill the air with their brazen sounds and fires are lit all around. The frightened animals try to escape by the way left open to them and are easily shot down. The booty is then equally divided among all the villagers.

Another way of capturing wild animals is by traps, consisting of circular pieces of wood with spikes all round, which are placed over holes dug in the ground and covered with earth or snow. The spikes point inwards, but are not in the plane of the circle, so that the rings placed properly will allow the feet of unweary animals to get in, but not to get out. The trap is secured by a rope, and when an animal has been caught, the huntsman who is watching close by comes up and dispatches him.

Fox hunting is carried on on horseback. In order to entice the foxes out of their holes the horns of animals are burnt, and the smell soon brings them out. They are then chased on horseback, and when tired out are struck down with Polo-sticks.

9

Hares are hunted in the same way, but the smell of the burnt horn does not attract them as it does the foxes. Both foxes and hares are hunted more easily when snow lies soft and deep, as the animals are sooner tired out than when the snow is hard. While the men chase the animals from one place to another, the women folk come out on the balconies of their houses to enjoy the sight; if a huntsman comes to grief, they give vent to their feelings—we know not whether of joy or sorrow—by freely abusing him. Pheasants are captured in the same way. There are few trees in Tibet, and they do not settle even on these, but live on the ground. They are hunted from one place to another on the snow until the cold and exhaustion make them unable to avoid the blow of the huntsman's stick. The snow-pheasant is caught by being inveigled into pits dug in snow. These are covered with sticks and have the appearance of little pools of water. The snow-pheasant in search of water descends from the mountains and settles on the pit. The sticks give away he tumbles in, and the snow coming down over him makes it impossible for him to fly.

In order to realise the possibility of hunting in the above manner, it should be understood that both men and women are expert riders. From their earliest years they are trained to feats of horsemanship which would do credit to professional performers. They mount and dismount with ease while the horse is at full speed, and hit with their arrows objects which they pass by in their career. They load and fire their matchlocks with surprising rapidity, having to do this a certain number of times within a certain space while galloping at full speed. With all the practice which a Tibetan goes through as a matter of course he eventually becomes an expert rider and a patient and persevering huntsman.

The game of polo as it is played by the Western Tibetans is especially suited to their natural taste. The game itself has not all the interest and variety of the English game as played in India, but there is as much dash and go in the one as in the other.

Cricket, lawn-tennis and football have been introduced by the writer of these pages in the town of Leh. It may be confidently expected that in a few years these games will reach the city of Lhassa.

The great winter amusement of skating is also a favourite pastime. Women and girls do not skate: indeed they do not take part in any of the sports we have just detailed, one reason being that they are more industrious than the sterner sex, and are content with taking a passive interest in them as spectators. Besides skating, sledging on the ice is indulged in by people living near the banks of rivers. In the spring when the hard snow becomes soft on the banks, huge masses of it are pushed into the current, and on these the people sit and drift down the river till the mass has diminished to such an extent that to proceed further would be dangerous.

Tibetans are fond of dancing. Contrary to the ideas prevalent in oriental countries, it is here thought no shame to dance: it is not relegated by the higher classes as in India, to a class of people who by profession lead shameless lives. Everyone is at liberty to trip it on the light fantastic too except the members of the royal family. These refrain from the pastime more perhaps as a matter of etiquette than because it is prohibited to them. Nothing pleases a father more than to see his daughter dancing better than the rest of the party. He lustily claps his hands and cries "bravo" with as little reserve as possible and as much delight as he is capable of. Their dancing is by no means attractive, though they are dressed out in all their finery, bedecked with jewels and their faces for once washed and clean : yet their movements are lifeless, the singing and music are no better than noise, and to an Indian who has seen the practised and graceful movements of the dancing girls of India the whole performance seems to be more suited to an expression of grief and sorrow than a manifestation of joy. Those who understand the language say that the songs are marked by a surpassing intensity of feeling and stirring pathos—but of both the matter and the language the writer knows too little to be able to advance any opinion. To him, therefore, the sense is lost on unintelligent ears.

Holiday making is as much a feature of life in Tibet as anywhere else. Spring is the time for picnicing, but what is peculiar about these Tibetan picnic is that men go out by them selves and women by themselves. It has already been mentioned that cleanliness is not one of the Tibetan virtues, and that he is expected to wash but once a year. It is perhaps when he goes out for his annual picnic that he is expected to do so.

According to what the writer ascertained from people of Lhassa, the city possesses a number of theatres. These owe their existence chiefly to the presence there of the Chinese They do not act plays, the theatres serve as concert halls. A number of people dressed up in various costumes, representing for instance, Chinamen, Tibetans, Englishmen and others come forward on the stage, wearing masks. A cymbal, drum and trumpet make up the musical portion of the programme. All the performers remain standing, one of their number comes forward and sings a song, a love song generally, or a comic or national song. He then goes back to his place, and is followed by another. If a Lama comes forward he generally sings a song of which the moral is : "Support your Lamas, be obedient to them and show hospitality to all pilgrims." Pilgrims are generally Lamas, so that the whole moral is give all you can to Lamas.

Gymnastic exercises are left to one class of people; to wandering beggars who thrive by such exhibitions. One trick of these men is to apply the somewhat blunt point of a sword to the navel, the handle resting on the ground, and to balance the body and turn it round in a horizontal plane. It is, of course, pretended that the point of the sword is not blunt : this is not so in reality; sometimes the skin is protected by a small plate of metal. Another trick which these men perform is to split in two a very heavy long stone, lying across the belly of a sleeping man, by hurling another stone against the centre. It seems a somewhat dangerous method of entertaining, and this impression is increased by the behaviour of the performers who solemnly offer prayers before attempting the trick. The long flat stone weighs as much as 1,200 lbs., and it is not easy to see how the thing is so neatly done. All the bystanders reward these performers who are sometimes Lamas very liberally for their services : something must always be given by everyone; the poorest if he can give nothing else gives at least a sewing needle, the property of his wife; the richer ones in addition to what they give, bid for the two pieces of stone and carry them away to their homes as sacred objects.

In addition to their tricks, these wandering performers do a kind of skirt dance accompanied with prayers. The order in which these acrobats go through their performances is ordinary gymnastic feats, skirt dance, sword dance, and stone trick, so that the most impressive trick is reserved for the end and this ingenuity and artfulness brings in a plentiful harvest, for they go home rich in money and kind.

We now come to the festivals. The greatest festival of the year is the "Lousar" or New Year's Day. The mention of this festival leads us to describe how Tibetans reckon their time. The year is divided into twelve months, every third year an extra month being added. The months of an ordinary year are supposed to contain 30 days each, but really contain only about 27 or 28; Tibetans, however, reckon these 28 days as thirty, and explain the difficulty by saying that certain days are lost, as many days as the number by which the month falls short of the thirty. The ordinary people compute periods of time by cycles of twelve years. Each one of these twelve years is known by the name of some animal, the first for instance, is year, the second ox year, the third tiger year, and so on through horse, dragon, serpent, hare, sheep, ape, bird, dog and hog. In books writers go by cycles of sixty years. Owing to the fact that every three years, the year has an extra month, the New Year's Day falls sometimes in the middle of our December, sometimes in January or February. As among Christians, so also among the Tibetans this day is one of peace and good will, when enemies are reconciled to one another, and friends strengthen the ties which bind them, by paying and receiving visits, "drinking chhang" to wish each other welfare and luck and by various other good offices. Betrothals are announced at this season of merriment, and the family meal gives way to a banquet such as the Tibetan loves to partake of. Here is served out the dish of the season; sausages made of "sattoo." This unlovely dish is prepared in a way disgusting to the refined palate of civilised nations, but its appearance is greeted with as much delight by young Tibetan as the appearance of the plum pudding is greeted by English children. The festival lasts five days. On the last day every family and every monastery lights as many lamps of oil as its means will allow, a custom which recalls the Hindu festival of *Devali*. On this day the headman of the village, or the prince of the place makes a sheaf of twigs and sets it on fire. An attendant then takes a sword and strikes the sheaf twice or thrice, symbolising the killing of the devil, or a Tibetan analogy to the Christian "the putting away of the old man." The burning sheaf is then carried out and every villager brings his own bundle of twigs and lights it from the sheaf. A procession is then formed, and they all proceed to some place outside the village, and there throw away on some spot the burning twigs. This burning of twigs reminds one of the Hindu festival of *Holi*, when wood and cowdung cakes go to make bonfires. At this season it is a religious duty with the Hindoos to become lascivious and obscene, and it is usual to indulge in the license of throwing dirt and red paint at one another: this license finds in a way its counterpart in Tibet. The young generation amuse themselves for four days with burning a kind of dry shrub obtained from the hill sides. They are allowed to abuse one another, and they generally form into parties to do so. On the last day after all the burning bundles have been thrown into the fields, the youths invade the town and levy contributions in money and kind on all the inhabitants; many, who are unable to satisfy their demands, close their doors against the young blackmailers, and find that they are irritated, and their houses pelted with stones.

Shoopla is the harvest festival. It is celebrated in the month of August or September. It is a day of merriment as well as of thanksgiving. After the prayer of thanksgiving has been offered up at the monastery, the harvest dance takes place. Two men, with the aid of a mask and sheet, form themselves into the figure of a lion. The first man has the mask representing the lion : his feet serve as its fore-paws. The second bends his back so as to form, as it were, the saddle part of the lion's back, and his feet serve as the lion's hind paws. A sheet is then thrown over the two, and the figure formed has indeed a suggestion of the lion. The tail is done up by a third man, who collects up the ends of the sheet behind. Men and women dance round this figure, and are eagerly watched by the simple folk who have come from many a mile around.

CHAPTER XIII.

CURIOUS CUSTOMS.

To say "good morning" or "thank you" is not with the Tibetan a mere matter of words. It is something more; it requires certain acts, acts which are quite in keeping with the fantastic character of the country. They use the same form of expression and action both for "thank you" and "good morning." To do either of these in the acknowledged style, a Tibetan has to say the word "jooly," and at the same time inclines his head slightly and put out his tongue. In society when chhang or tea drinking is going on, a Tibetan has occasion to exhibit his tongue pretty frequently a practice which in Europe would have been very welcome to the doctors. By the frequent use of this mode of bidding the time and saying "thank you" nature itself has come so well to the aid of the nomadic tribes that they have, as it were, invented a means to economise labour, and one always sees them with their tongues out. In Kham—a district to the North-East in addition to the lolling out of the tongue—it is usual to bid the time by turning up the thumb of the left hand (which is a dire insult to the Indian). In other districts the fashion is to take hold of the left ear.

Women have another way of doing these things. They cross their hands with the closed fists, so that the bangles touch one another, and then bring the right hand thrice to the forehead, saying "jooly" every time and making a slight courtesy each time. One formality of Tibetan etiquette is peculiarly interesting. It is absolutely indispensable when one rich man visits another or when invitations to a marriage, birth or funeral feast are accepted. This is the presentation of a scarf of salutation and prevails only among the men. A *makpa* husband has to present it to his father-in-law, a friend to the father of a child on the occasion of the birth-feast. The mode of presenting this scarf differs with the rank of the persons concerned. If a man of inferior rank in life visits one of higher rank, the former must throw the scarf about the feet of the latter; if, however, the visitor is the equal or superior of the person he visits, he throws the scarf about the neck. In this way many scarfs are used up, but as visits are paid and repaid, this practice is not a costly one for the well-to-do, and the poor are required to do it only on the occasions mentioned. A scarf of salutation must also accompany every letter written by one Tibetan to another, otherwise the latter will indignantly refuse it. The Tibetans have evidently a strict code of etiquette, and their rules are perhaps not so fine and exacting as those which are recognised among civilised races, but they mean to abide by the few rules they have imposed on themselves. A scarf is used also on a certain other occasion, when tea is being served up to some high officer of state or to members of the royal family. The one who serves up the tea has to wind a scarf round his mouth, in order that no foul breath of his might pollute the tea he is offering to the august functionary.

The rules of good breeding and etiquette also require that in addressing persons of different rank or in speaking of the same thing when connected with difference of rank different words should be used. The Tibetan language is in a way very extensive ; for instance, speaking of the shoes of people of varying rank, although the shoes may be exactly similar, different expressions must be used. Speaking of the shoes of a prince "jufsha" is the right word, while "kufsha" is the word as applied to those of ordinary men. The eyes for instance, of the people are called "mig" and those of a prince or a big man "migma." Such distinctions are not confined to the instances quoted, they comprise a large number of objects. Among the traits of the Tibetans, which please an observer of their institutions and manners, the welcome offered to distinguished visitors travelling through the land, by the settled people, is a very noticeable feature. An official of high rank can be at once made out from his bearing and other marked characteristics, as, for instance, he is always preceded by a forerunner upon horseback, and is followed by a servant, who bears a banner, often inscribed with the name and rank of the dignitary. When the arrival of some person of importance, as for instance the headman of a village or some other officer, is announced, the women folk of the place which he is passing by turn out to present "sattoo" and "milk" and "chhang" to the traveller. In the sattoo, pencil cedar and incense sticks are burning and the traveller just touches the offerings and returns them. The musicians of the village too have turned out with their drums and flutes, and, with the best of intentions, they play what they think is music, which, begging their pardon. is in reality only a jarring noise. The Lamas in the monasteries too welcome the traveller with their trumpets and flutes and cymbals. Every village and every monastery greets him in this way, and at the place where he stops the headman of the village, or of the monastery if the traveller puts up at the monastery, gets up a feast in his honour. The whole journey therefore becomes what may be called a "royal" progress, it being the business of each village to send on the news of the dignitary's arrival to the next in order that he may be fittingly received.

There is a curious custom among those people worth mentioning, the like of which is hardly to be found in any other nation. So soon as a grandson or granddaughter is born to the head of the family, the whole burden of the family devolves upon the son, and the headman with his mate retires to a place set apart for the purpose to lead a life of voluntary renunciation, and henceforth he resigns all affairs to the care of his son, who becomes at once the headman. I have seen with my own eyes the Raja Moths to thus relinquish his estate while in the full enjoyment of his physical powers in favour of his son. The good of it is, the heirs have no occasion to be tired of their parents to wait and wait for independent charge till death removes the incumbent. If there be *several fathers*, they all abdicate for the sake of their common and joint offspring.

Before concluding it must be said that Tibetans make use of a language of flowers. They also fix flowers in their caps and upon their breasts by means of needles. The flowers in this land are very scarce, and they therefore make use of bright and many coloured leaves of trees instead to decorate their persons, and use them in the way the English coxcomb do the flowers in the button-holes. Although among the Tibetans the same ideas regarding love and love-making do not prevail, which are so well known here, yet lovers often have recourse to flowers to give expression to their sentiments. When one person sends another a bunch of yellow flowers, he virtually confesses that the other person is as dear to him as gold—as intense a degree of love as the Tibetan is capable of. or imagines he is capable of, because he is second to no one in the world for his love of gold. If the flowers sent are red, the colour of blood, the message is as it were a denunciation of the cruelty of the person to whom the flowers are sent; if the flowers sent are blue, it indicates a consciousness on the part of the sender that he or she is an object of love to the one to whom they are sent. But if an unfortunate maid or swain suffers from a broken heart, he or she sends the tidings to the other party in the form of a bisected leaf; but if the bunch is made up of all the tree varieties of flowers just mentioned, and it contains in addition a piece of burnt wood, it is a message condemning the unfaithfulness of the other party, which has burnt the heart of the sender.

It will be seen that the colours to represent the different feelings of love or hatred are well chosen, and not, as I am told, in the case of England by mere convention or associating different flowers with certain ideas and sentiments. If the Tibetans had a great number of flowers, they would perhaps have made a very sensible language. They have few, but they use them in a simple practical way.

And so it is that the Tibetans manage to play the "pranks" of civilisation in the department of love, while in the others they are notoriously behind every section of the human race.

CHAPTER XIV.

WHY FOREIGNERS ARE FORBIDDEN TO ENTER TIBET.

I have had occasion to allude to the reasons which induce the Tibetans to exclude foreigners from the country. The subject requires wider treatment than has been hitherto possible and I propose to inquire into the causes which had made Lassa till last year the most impenetrable country in the world. Tibetans are in a somewhat vague and undefined manner acquainted with the might and power of the Europeans, who rule on the other side of the Himalayah. From time to time native travellers from the north of India, from Kashmir Nepal and Bhutan have crossed the Himalayah and borne the news of the rise and progress of the new empire in India. They have seen this power advance little by little towards their own borders. Like the wild Afghan tribes, who have been the cause of so much trouble to the Indian Government, Tibetans have learned to regard the presence of this powerful neighbour as a possible source of danger to their independence. Apathetic though they are, when their feelings are worked upon by the power-loving Lamas, they find motives strong enough to stir whatever feelings of political independence they may possess and assist the authorities in their efforts to exclude all foreigners from the land.

When Zorawar Singh after a short campaign took Leh, the Kashmir Government allowed sportsmen to shoot at certain seasons in the territory it had acquired. In consequence of this concession Ladakh soon became a favourite shooting ground for sportsmen from Kashmir and India. The very fact of the introduction of the revolutionizing breechloader, immeasureably superior to the flint lock of the natives, produced an impression of awe and fear which quickly found its way to Lassa and made the authorities all the more resolved to exclude people possessing such dreadful weapons from the country. It must be remembered that ever since 1720 there have been two representatives of China called "Ambans" at the court of Lassa. They imbibe the prejudices of their countrymen, and, being well acquainted with the aggressive policy of European nations, no doubt foster the anti-European feelings of Tibetans, who are more willing to follow blindly than to think for themselves. In 1865, the then Grand Lama of Tibet directed the Emperor of China to prohibit any European entering Tibet.

The Lamas work upon the religious feelings of the Tibetans by ascribing all the evils which befall the country to the laxity which is displayed in keeping away foreigners. The Dalai" Lamas or Grand Lamas when elected are minors, boys four years old, and when they are just of age and are entitled to manage the affairs of the country by themselves, they always die or rather they are poisoned by the Regent who has been entrusted with the supreme power during their minority. The Tibetan, however, does not suspect any foul play and the Regent makes use of their credulity to shield himself by attributing their deaths to the fact that foreigners have been permitted to enter the land. When the Grand Lama, directed the Emperor of China to exclude fereigners from Tibet, he urged it on the ground that ever since the white missionaries and others had been visiting the land women have become unfaithful to their husbands, and the people wavered in their allegiance to the established religion.

The instructions issued by the authorities of Lassa to the headman of the village and local petty chiefs are very stringent. One of the conditions under which all of them invariably hold their posts is that they will allow no foreigners to pass through their district; offences against this order being liable to punishment by death. But when they find that travellers cannot be induced to change their purpose and leave Tibet, the usual course is to set them on a track which gives Lassa a wide berth, information of their arrival being sent to the next village so that every precaution is taken to direct travellers by a road leading away as widely as possible from the sacred city. Thus it is that the local chiefs and guardians, who according to the precepts of their religion are not allowed to destroy life in whatever form, evade the law and form a brotherhood as it were, to shield themselves from the effects of such offences.

Modern European travellers are recognised at once unless disguised with more than ordinary care. The caravans, which contain their provisions and clothes and other necessaries of life, are unusually large for people whose object is not trade; they always want grain—a commodity which it is by no means easy to procure, and which even when procured has been with difficulty obtained for the money. Guns too form a necessary article of every traveller's outfit, and the shooting of wild animals and winged birds near monasteries is distasteful to the Tibetan mind. Almost every caravan of a European traveller carrying guns is supposed to be the small advance guard of a huge army that is behind; no wonder that the Tibetan try in their ignorance to keep away all white men.

Another cause of irritation is the employment of Arghons as servants and guides. It must be remembered that the Oriental imagination, highly strung by the tales, legends and beliefs which it has had to swallow during all the years of its existence draws gigantic conclusions from the most insignificant premises. The Arghons as a class are not liked by the Tibetans; they are Mahomedans by religion and easily induce Tibetan women to become Mahomedan and contract monogamous or polygamous marriages with them. They increase in numbers far more rapidly than the pure population. For these two reasons the secular and spiritual authorities do not regard the half-castes with feelings of kindness; the secular, because they rightly fear that over-population will bring misery and poverty on the people; the spritual, because every woman who marries an Arghon is one member lost to their religion. Now European travellers as a rule engage Arghons in their service. They are a deceitful and cunning lot, as ill-bred half-castes all over the world generally are. They know well how to curry favour with their masters, and do not hesitate to obtain by force and without payment whatever their masters require. Redress is not possible because the timid Tibetans are threatened with further ill-treatment should they complain. Cases have also occurred in which these Arghons have secretly injured the interest of their masters while pretending to serve them. A European traveller's mules were once stolen away at the request and by the connivance of the Arghons as they feared detection and punishment by the Lassa officials. Such deeds do not win for these time-serving rogues the good will of the Tibetans, and they remain a hated lot ; and somehow or other this association of the white man with the Arghons is a source of irritation to the illogical Tibetan ; in his mind perhaps he sets down the Europeans as a class of men one degree more wicked even if a great deal wealthier than their hated guides.

CHAPTER XV.

HISTORY OF THE BUDDHIST RELIGION IN TIBET.

The religion of Tibet is interesting not only in itself, on account of its quaint belief and its still quainter ceremonies. It is indeed very remarkable how Buddhism in developing into Lamaism has accomplished in many respects the same transformations in Tibet, that Christianity accomlished in medæval Europe. This is quite evident from the chief features of the creed and cult known as Lamaism (from the word Lama, the name for a priest). To understand Lamaism, we must explain here in as brief a way as possible the fundamental doctrines and principles which Buddha is supposed to have enunciated. There is so much ignorance—now however, rapidly disappearing—among the majority of non-Buddhists as to what Buddha actually taught that it is necessary to say a few words on the subject. "Buddha" is a word meaning "enlightened" and the real name of the founder of the religion which goes by the man of Buddhism was Siddhartha. Gautama was the family name.

What then did Buddha or the 'enlightened one' teach? First let it be known that Buddha entirely ignored the questions of the existence of God and of an individual immortal soul in every human being. Buddha only believed in the material world; he thought that it was fruitless to discuss the two points—whether there is a God, or whether human beings have souls.

He was therefore in plain language an agnostic. A great deal of all the knowledge that a non-Buddhist has about Siddhartha's teaching is associated with the term Nirvan or annihilation. This indeed is the great goal which was to be aimed at by all his disciples. It meant simply extinction of passions, of all those feelings of anger, vanity, impurity and pride which make men unhappy. Once these were extinguished, bliss, repose, content would be the lot of every individual in whom that consummation had taken place

Gautama pointed out that the only path to Nirvana was by "right views, right thought right speech, right actions, right living, right exertion, right recollection and right meditations." He calls thus the noble eightfold path by which man might hope to attain eternal rest.

Gautama called to men to follow an ascetic life, and the Order which he founded was a natural outcome of his views of life. Existence is bound up with evil ; those passions which bring life into existence and tend to maintain it, also bring evil and decay. You must strike at existence itself. All those who were eager to find the solution of the problem of life were to lead ascetic lives, removed from temptations and passions. But all lay people might hope to attain Nirvana, by practicing self-culture not in their life however, but in another life. By a gradual process of purification, one existence would become more holier than another, and enlightenment be made easier of attainment. There was thus a twofold standard of human conduct —one for those who trusted to attain "Nirvana" in their present existence; another for those who were content to attain it after many new births. Now as the best authorities deny that Buddha believed in or taught the existence of an individual soul, it would seem that Buddha meant by transmigration, simply the progress of the race, that the term simply expresses the continuation of a man's life in that of his children, so that if it be true agnostics and rationalists have great reason for glorifying as they do.

Buddha, as we are told, lived in B. C. 500. Soon after his death a great number of legends and supernatural events began to be associated with his life and teachings, and his simple teaching of the system of self-culture became tangled in a mass of observances. In the first century of the Christian era, that is after an existence of 600 years there came a split in Buddhism. Buddhists grouped themselves into two rival schools; one called their system "Mahayana" the other "Himayana" the Great vehicle, and the Little vehicle, respectively. The followers of the Great Vehicle were the Buddhists of the north the followers of the Little Vehicle were those of Ceylon, Burma and Siam.

The northern Buddhists differed from those of the south in laying greater stress on that virtue, which is content with looking to "Nirvana" or extinction after many countless new births. It did not deny that a man might become a "Buddha" in the first stage of his existence, so that it did not contradict the teachings of the southern school; but it laid greater stress on that virtue which did not seek to accomplish all at once.

Now when a man tried the more ascetic course, the course which led to deliverance from evil here, he was an "Arahat"—if he tried to obtain deliverance only gradually he became a "Buddhist." A "Buddhisat" became more "important" than an Arahat, and if any great religious teacher appeared at any time, he was supposed to have been in previous birth a Buddhist, and after his death he was worshipped as a Buddha. But the southern school, though its disciples have given up the attempt to become "Arahats," is still subject to his " Himayana" system, restricting salvation to the comparatively few.

The next development of Buddhism took place in the sixth century when the 'yoga' cult of the Brahmans was assimilated by the degenerating Buddhism of northern India. Rites and incantations and charms were the new growths. Tantrism, devil worship, magic and witchcraft came in to destroy every trace of Buddha's grand teaching. The special feature of this Tantrism was that it gave the Buddhist wives, and introduced fiends and fiendesses who were to be worshipped. This was the religion introduced into Tibet in the seventh century of the Christian era. What the Lamas retain to some extent is the correct idea of the true teaching of Buddha with respect to life, and is clear from the existence in the monastries of the pictorial wheel of life. It is ascribed to Buddha himself. In the rim of this wheel, are shown the several stages through which an individual life passes until in the last he dies. The first stage is represented by a blind she-*Camel* led by a driver and is intended to symbolise the unconscious life of the infant. In the next link or stage, the unconscious will is performed and shaped for individual existence; just as clay in the hands of the potter. The rise of consciousness is the next stage, and shows a monkey becoming a man. The fourth stage is represented either by a physician feeling the pulse of a patient, or a man crossing an ocean. This is to the rise of individual consciousness. The rise of the understanding is the next step in life, and is represented in the fifth picture by a pair of eyes gleaming through a mark.

The next step is contact ; and contact brings feelings of pain or pleasure. Contact is represented by people kissing and feeling by an arrow entering the eye. Feeling brings desire and this is represented by a man drinking wine. Greed is the next advance on desire ; and this is representend by a man plucking fruits and gathering them in a basket. The tenth stage shows us a woman and typifies that state of greed, which leads to marriage. In the next picture, a woman is giving birth to a child, and now the man whose history has been traced is in possession of an heir. And the last stage is represented by a dead body borne on the back of an individual—this is Death.

PICTURES OF TIBETAN LIFE

A COLLECTION OF SKETCHES

MADE BY

Rev. Ahmad Shah

DURING HIS TOUR IN TIBET.

CONTENTS.

	Plate.
The Origin of the Creation. A representation of the five species that are considered to have been created first, others having sprung from them.	... 1
The people of Lower Tibet.	... 2
A Tibetan lady on her Journey preceded by a servant.	... 3
(MALE ATTIRE).—1. Boots. 2. A coat. 3. A girdle. 4. A hat. 5. A cap. 6. A Raja's cap. 7. A cap. 8. A cap. 9. A money bag. 10. A handkerchief folded.	... 4
(FEMALE ATTIRE).—1. Shawl. 2, 4. Ear rings. 3. Skirt. 5. Brass shield. 6. Money bags. 7. Boots.	... 5
1. A tobacco Pouch. 2. A shell bungle. 3. A tinder box. 4. A table. 5. A tea cup. 6. A Sauce pan. 7. A tea pot. 8. A wooden vessel. 9. A bag.	... 6
1. Ear flaps. 2. An ornament. 3. A brass shield with money bags hanging from it. 4. A head dress. 5. Ear rings. 6. Felt boots. 7. A locket.	... 7
1. A money bag. 2. A Folded handkerchief. 3. A locket. 4. Necklaces. 5. A shawl. 6. A shell bungle. 7. A locket. 8. A silver bracelet. 9. A silver ornament.	... 8
1. A pen case. 2. A book packed up 3, 4. Knife and sheath. 5. A finger ring. 6, 7. Lockets for head dress. 8. A Jug. 9. A water bottle. 10. An Ink-pot. 11. Amulet in which Buddha's image is carried about.	... 9
1. Stove and kettle. 2. A spoon. 3. Sauce-pot on fire. 4. Tea-pot on fire. 5. Ale-pot.	... 10
1. Sword. 2. Knives in a sheath. 3. Reaping instrument. 4. Flute. 5. Tea churner's case 6. Pipes.	... 11
A Wedding Ceremony.	... 12
1. Seat for guests. 2. Ale pots. (*a*) Dough for refreshment. 3. Ladies ready for dancing.	... 13
1. A wedding feast. 2. A bride's maid. 3. Bride. 4. Bridegroom. 5. Best men. 6. Ale pots. Bricks made of dough; these are distributed to every family members. 7. A band.	... 14
A gentleman on horseback.	... 15
1. A Rope maker. 2, 3. Weavers. 4. A Blanket maker.	... 16
Crossing a bridge.	... 17
1. Manufacturing Macroni. 2. Churning. 3. Tailors. 4. A customer trying his coat on	... 18

	Plate
1. Pack mules. 2. A nomad driving his loaded sheep and his watch dog.	... 19
Fishing.	... 20
1. A brigand attacking a trader. 2. A cooli. 3. Barter. 4. Weighing wool.	... 21
Ferry boats.	... 22
1. Ploughing and sowing. 2. Ink-pot. 3. Pouch for ink-pot. 4. A pen case. 5. Digging manure.	... 23
Carpenters at work.	... 24
1. Blacksmiths. 2. Carpenters.	... 25
Coppersmiths at work.	... 26
1. Rough outline of a model Tibetan house. 2. Agricultural implements.	... 27
1. A prince receiving salute from Lamas and his procession. 2. A prince and his courtiers.	... 28
1. Budha. 2. A devil made of sticks and strings to be burnt on their new years day 3. Mitre. 4. Wreath of a priest.	... 29
1. Chabbas or Tibetan traders. 2. Lamas. 3. A Nun of the red sect. 4. Nuns of the yellow sect.	... 30
1. Nomads paying their respects to a headman of the village. 2. Dictating from a manuscript.	... 31
A Lassa chief on his journey.	... 32
High Class Lassa Women.	... 33
1. Vessels containing sacred juice and sacred food 2. Mitre. 3. Cantaple or charten.	... 34
Articles belonging to the Budhists Altar.	... 35
Flags, Musical instruments and an incense burner.	... 36
1. Preaching from a picture. 2. Reading from a book. 3. Trimurti (A three headed image.) 4. Incense burner. 5. Image with eleven heads. 6. Budha.	... 37
1. Administering holy communion. 2. A palanquin carried by mules.	... 38
A Kushook (incarnation) blessing a passerby.	... 39
A funeral procession. 2. Writing a charm. 3. Physician and his patient. 4. Exorcising. 5. Lamas reading.	... 40
1. A skirt dance. 2. A Juggller breaking a stone. 3. Manufacturing tea into bricks.	... 41

PLATE 1

The origin of the creation. A representation of the five species that are considered to have been created first, others having sprung from them

PLATE 2

The people of Lower Tibet

PLATE 3

A Tibetan lady on her journey preceded by a servant

PLATE 4

(Male Attire)

1. Boots 2. A coat 3. A girdle 4. A hat 5. A cap 6. A Raja's cap 7. A cap 8. A cap 9. A money bag 10. A handkerchief folded

PLATE 5

(Female Attire)

1. Shawl 2 & 4. Ear rings 3. Skirt 5. Brass shield 6. Money bags 7. Boots

PLATE 6

1. A tobacco pouch 2. A shell bungel 3. A tinder box 4. A table 5. A tea cup 6. A sauce pan 7. A tea pot 8. A wooden vessel 9. A bag

PLATE 7

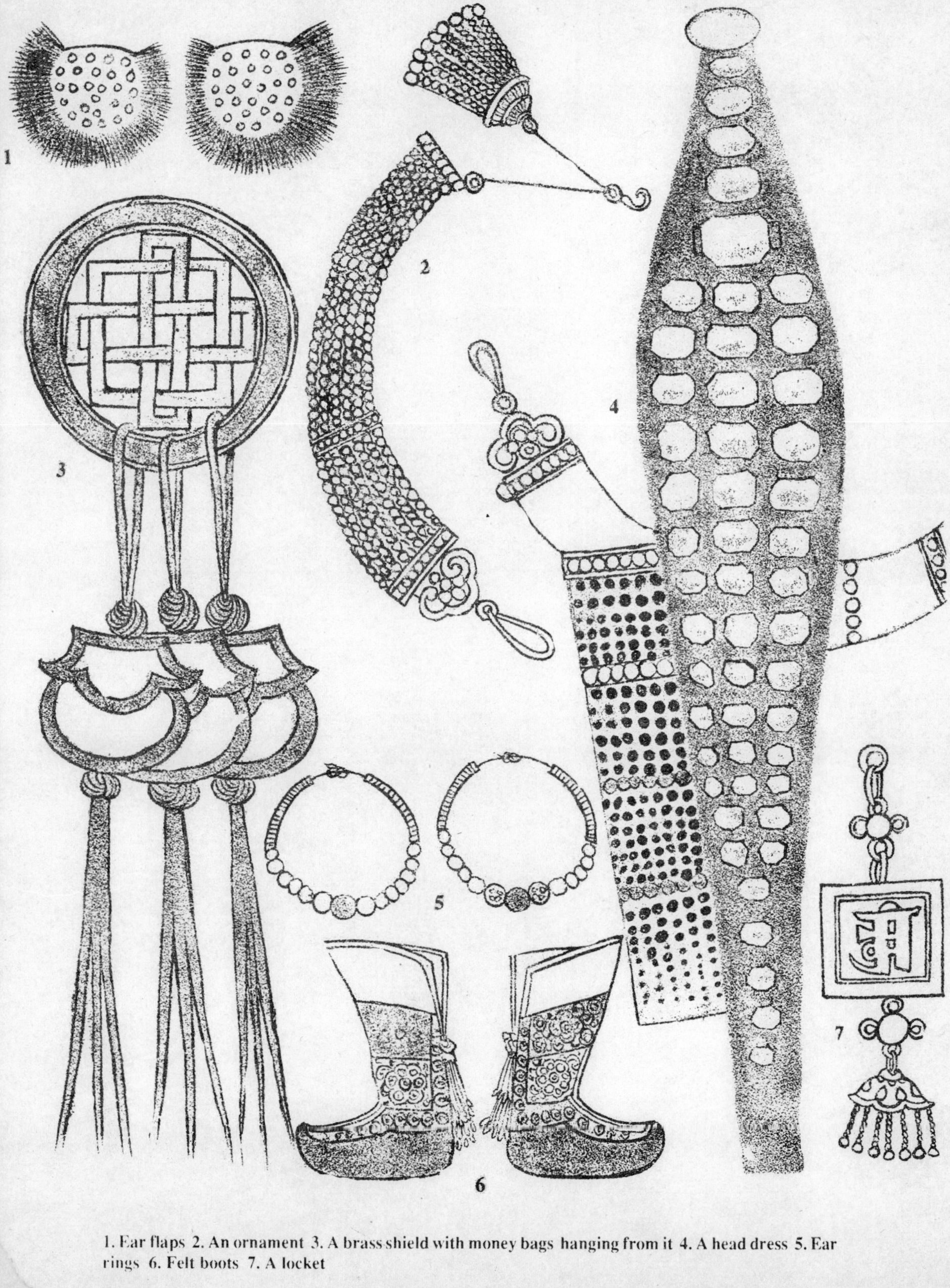

1. Ear flaps 2. An ornament 3. A brass shield with money bags hanging from it 4. A head dress 5. Ear rings 6. Felt boots 7. A locket

PLATE 8

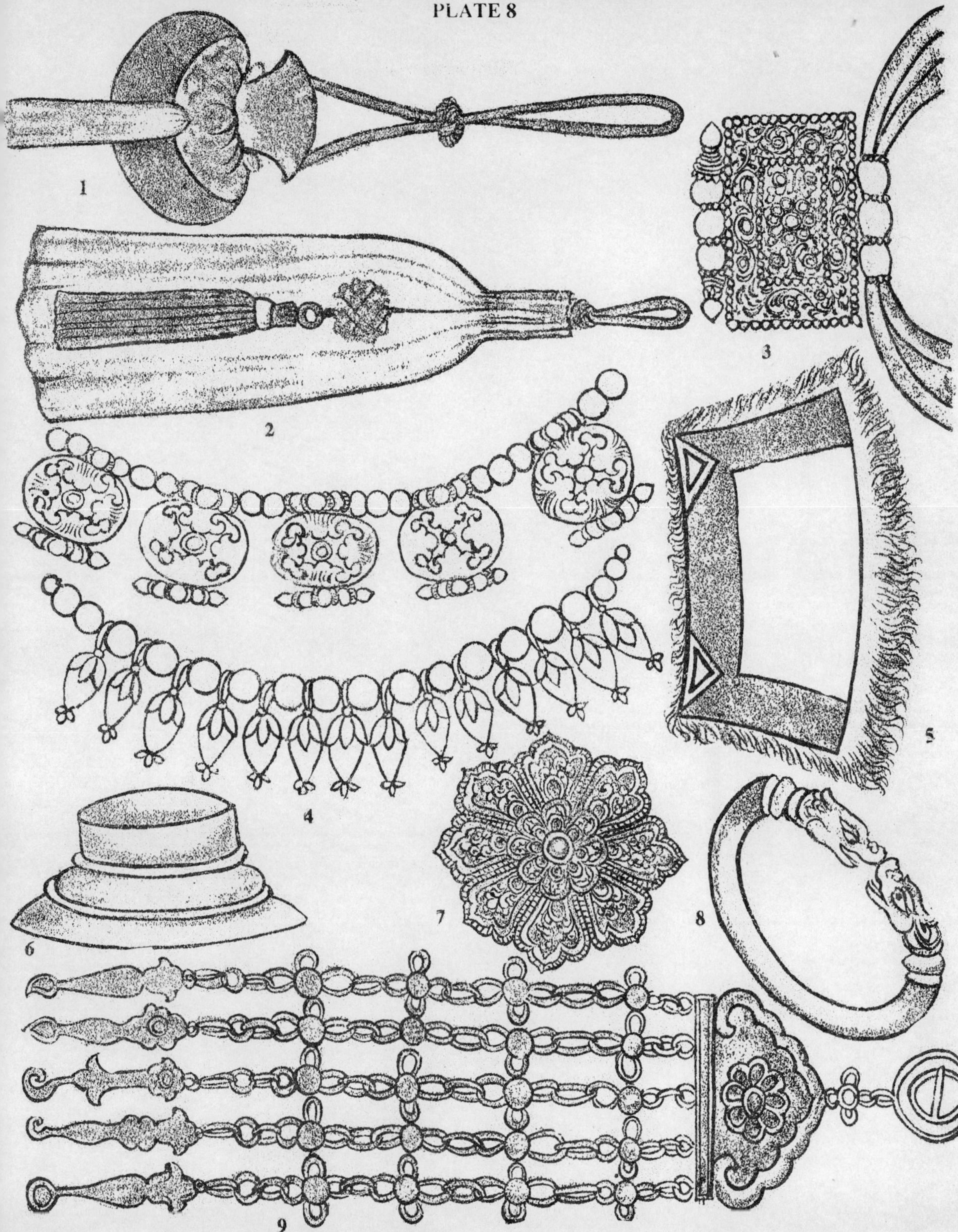

1. A money bag 2. Folded handkerchief 3. A locket 4. Necklaces 5. A shawl 6. A shell bungle 7. A locket 8. A silver bracelet 9. A silver ornament

PLATE 9

1. A pen case 2. A book packed up 3 & 4. Knife and sheath 5. A finger ring 6 & 7. Lockets for head dress 8. A jug 9. A water bottle 10. An ink-pot 11. Amulet in which Buddha's image is carried about

PLATE 10

1

2

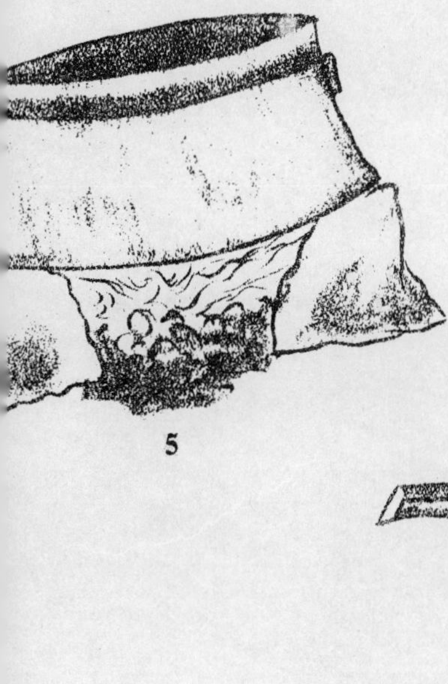

5

4

3

1. Stove and kettle 2. A spoon 3. Sauce pot on fire 4. Tea pot on fire 5. Ale pot

PLATE 11

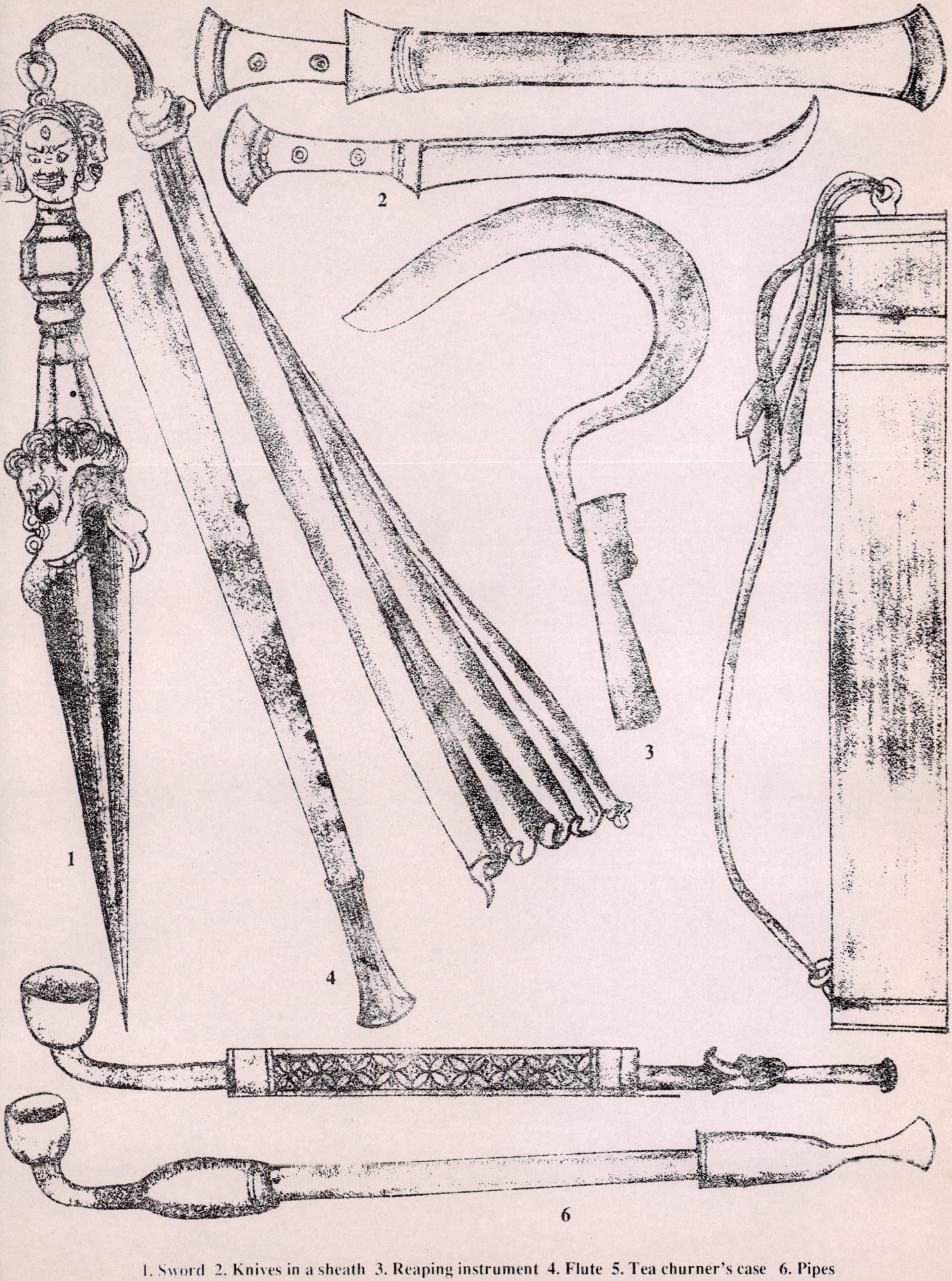

1. Sword 2. Knives in a sheath 3. Reaping instrument 4. Flute 5. Tea churner's case 6. Pipes

PLATE 12

A Wedding Ceremony

PLATE 13

1. Seat for guests 2. Ale pots (a) Dough for refreshment 3. Ladies ready for dancing

PLATE 14

1. A wedding feast 2. A bride's maid 3. Bride 4. Bridegroom 5. Best men 6. Ale pots; Bricks made of dough these are distributed to every family member 7. A band

PLATE 15

A gentlemen on horseback.

PLATE 16

1

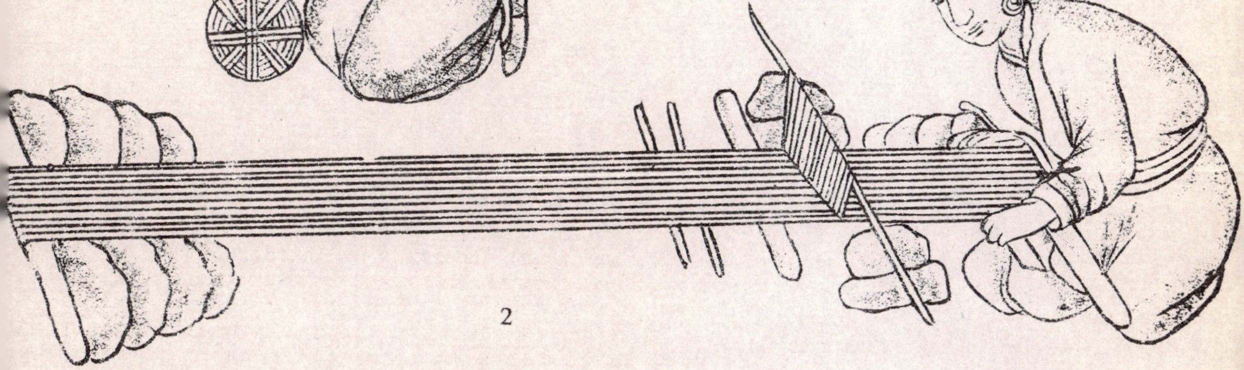

2

4

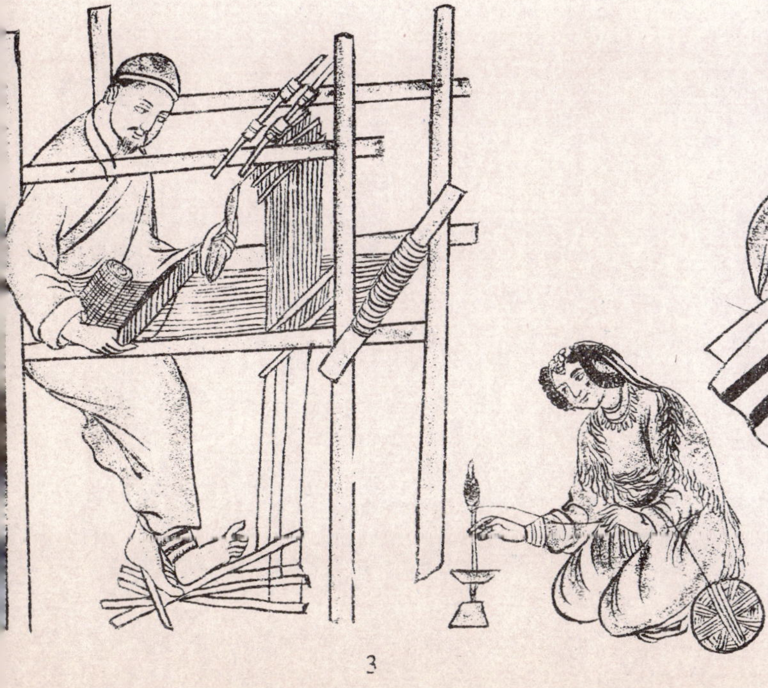

3

1. A rope maker 2 & 3 Weavers 4. A blanket marker

PLATE 17

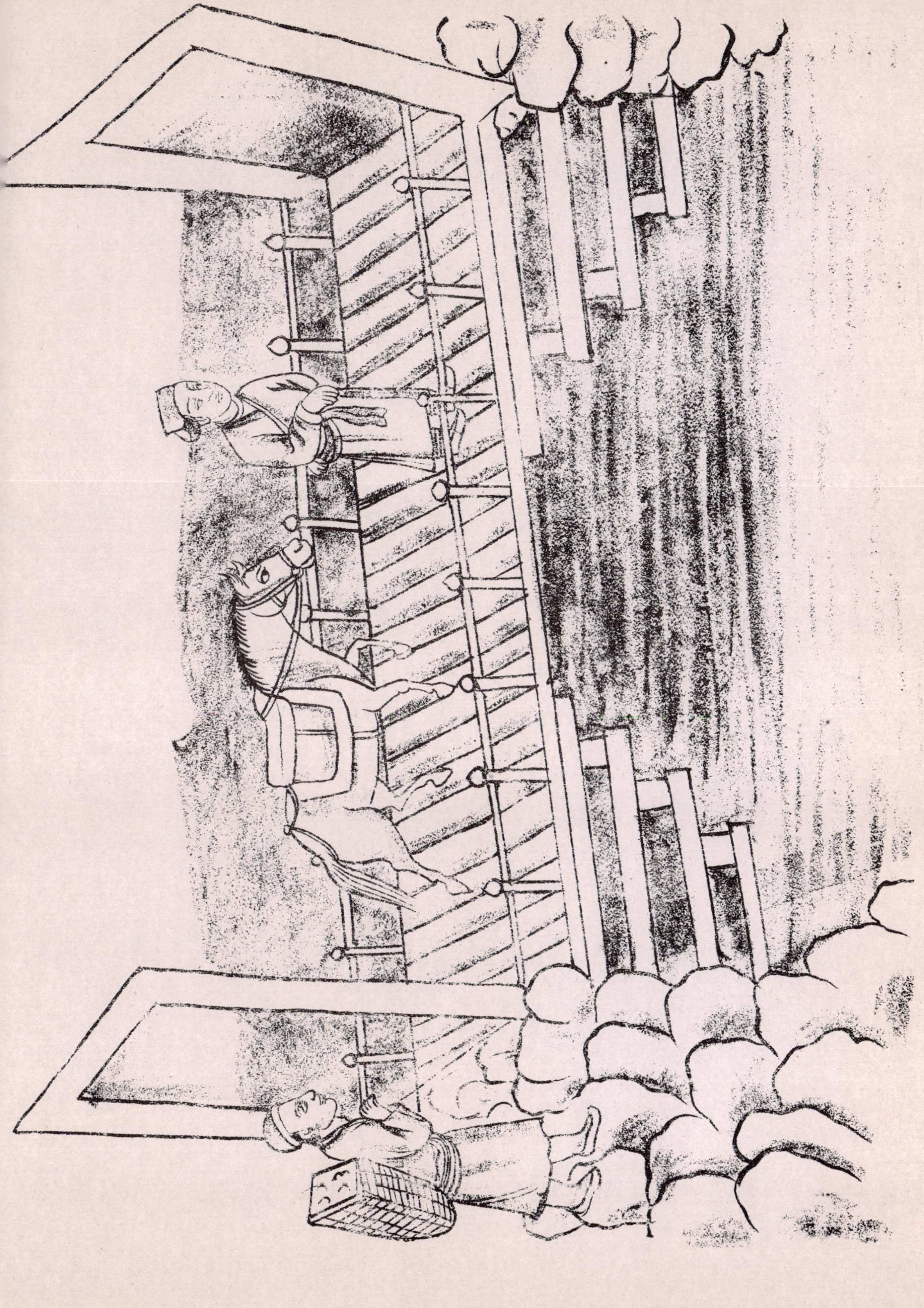

Crossing a bridge

1. Manufacturing Macroni 2. Churning 3. Tailors 4. A customer trying his coat on

PLATE 19

1. Pack mules 2. A Nomad driving his loaded sheep and his watch dog

PLATE 20

Fishing

PLATE 21

1. A brigand attacking a trader 2. A coolie 3. Barter 4. Weighing wool

PLATE 22

Ferry boats

PLATE 23

1. Ploughing and sowing 2. Ink pot 3. Pouch for ink pot 4. A pen case. 5. Digging manure.

PLATE 24

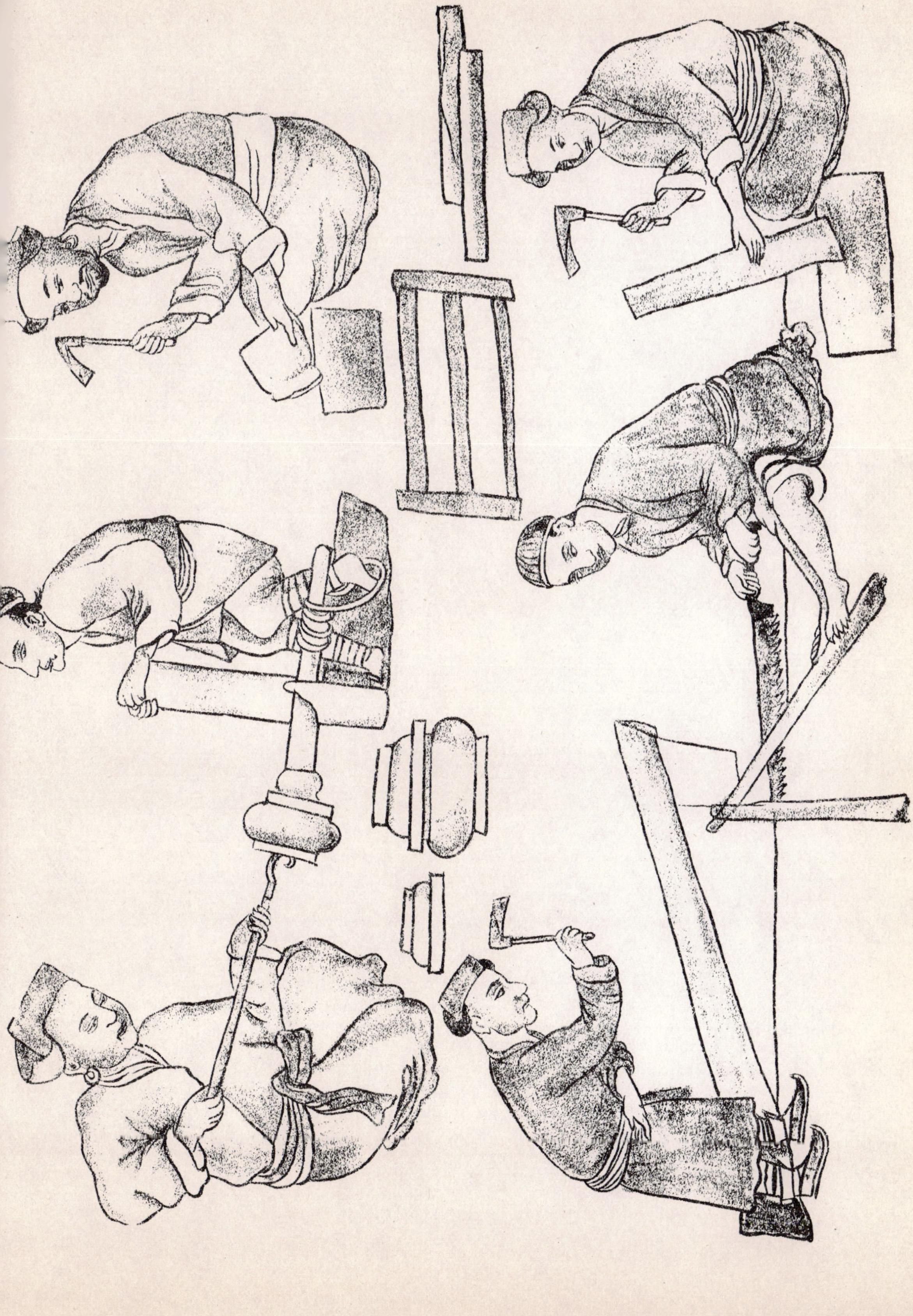

Carpenters at work

PLATE 25

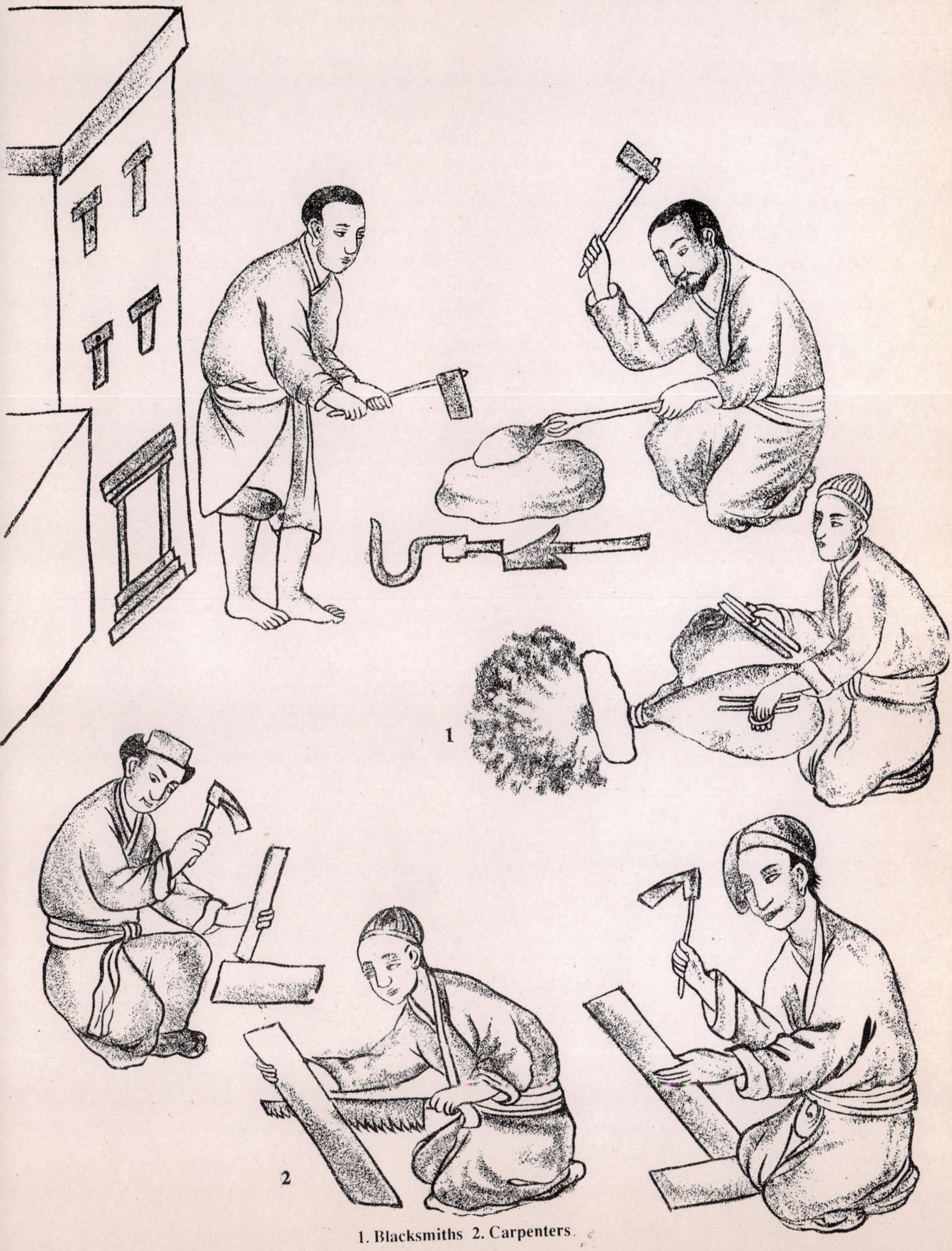

1. Blacksmiths 2. Carpenters

PLATE 26

Coppersmiths at work

PLATE 27

1

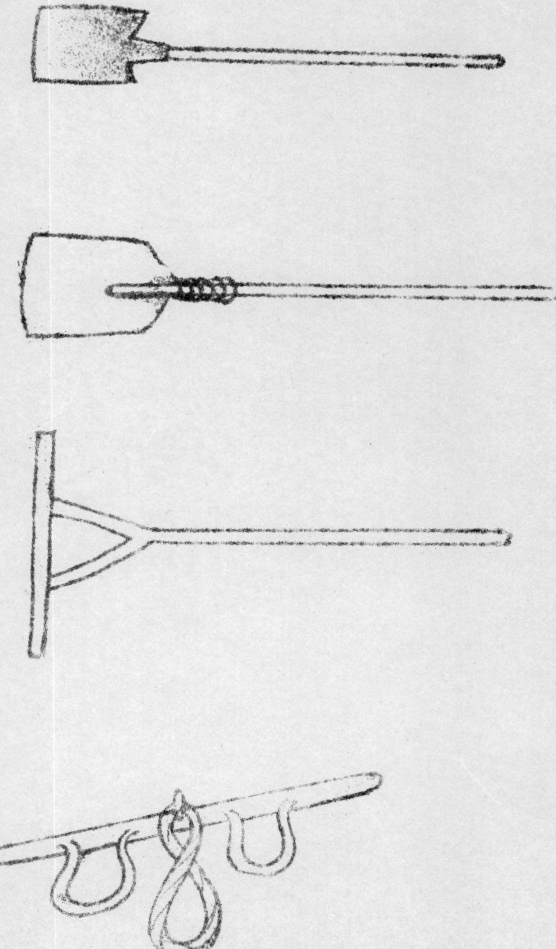

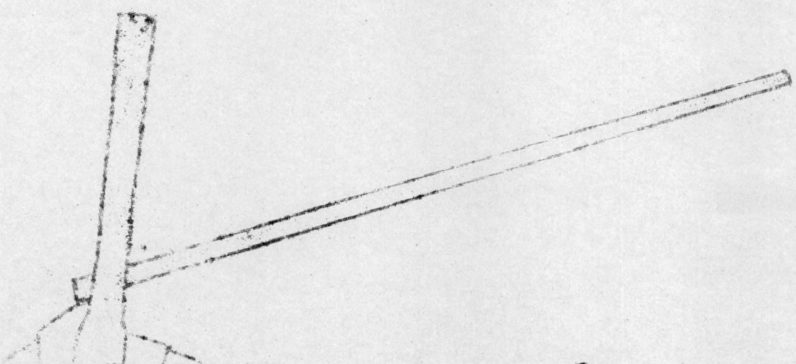

2

1. Rough outline of a model Tibetan house   2. Agricultural implements

PLATE 28

1. A prince receiving salute from Lamas and his procession   2. A prince and his courtiers

PLATE 29

. Buddha 2. A devil made of sticks and strings to be burnt on their New Year's day 3. Mitre. 4. Wreath
f a priest

PLATE 30

1. Chabbas or Tibetan traders 2. Lamas 3. A nun of the red sect 4. Nuns of the yellow sect.

PLATE 31

1

2

1. Nomads paying their respects to a headman of the village

2. Dictating from a manuscript

PLATE 32

A Lassa chief on his journey

PLATE 33

High class Lassa women

PLATE 34

1. Vessels containing sacred juice and sacred food 2. Mitre 3. Cantapie or charten.

PLATE 35

Articles belonging to the Buddhist altar

PLATE 36

Flags, musical instruments and an incense burner

PLATE 37

1. Preaching from a picture 2. Reading from a book 3. Trimurti (A three headed image) 4. Incense burner 5. Image with eleven heads 6. Buddha

PLATE 38

1

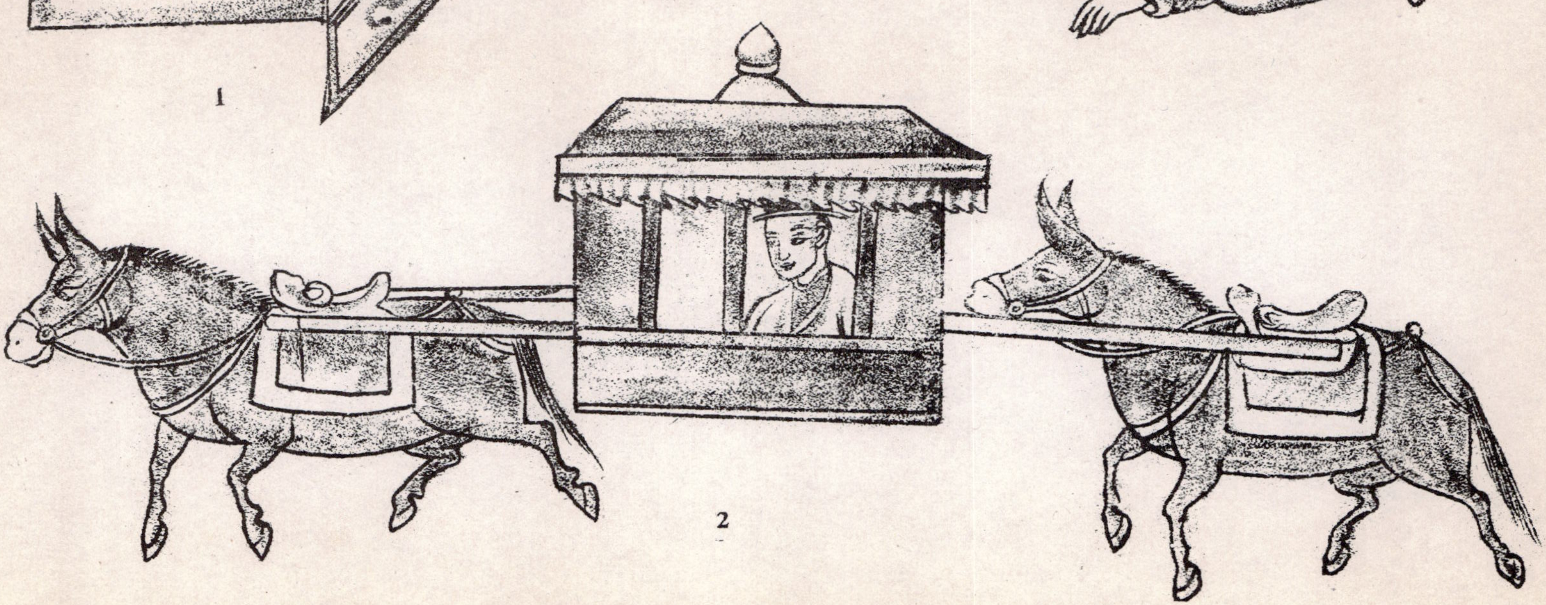

2

1. Administering holy eommunion 2. A palanquin carried by mules